Microsoft
explained

Books Available

By both authors:

BP327 DOS one step at a time
BP337 A Concise User's Guide to Lotus 1-2-3 for Windows
BP341 MS-DOS explained
BP346 Programming in Visual Basic for Windows
BP352 Excel 5 explained
BP362 Access one step at a time
BP387 Windows one step at a time
BP388 Why not personalise your PC
BP400 Windows 95 explained
BP406 MS Word 95 explained
BP407 Excel 95 explained
BP408 Access 95 one step at a time
BP409 MS Office 95 one step at a time
BP415 Using Netscape on the Internet*
BP420 E-mail on the Internet*
BP426 MS-Office 97 explained
BP428 MS-Word 97 explained
BP429 MS-Excel 97 explained
BP430 MS-Access 97 one step at a time
BP433 Your own Web site on the Internet
BP448 Lotus SmartSuite 97 explained
BP456 Windows 98 explained*
BP460 Using Microsoft Explorer 4 on the Internet*
BP464 E-mail and news with Outlook Express*
BP465 Lotus SmartSuite Millennium explained
BP471 Microsoft Office 2000 explained
BP472 Microsoft Word 2000 explained
BP473 Microsoft Excel 2000 explained
BP474 Microsoft Access 2000 explained
BP478 Microsoft Works 2000 explained

By Noel Kantaris:

BP258 Learning to Program in C
BP259 A Concise Introduction to UNIX*
BP284 Programming in QuickBASIC
BP325 A Concise User's Guide to Windows 3.1

Microsoft Word 2000 explained

by

N. Kantaris
and
P.R.M. Oliver

Bernard Babani (publishing) Ltd
The Grampians
Shepherds Bush Road
London W6 7NF
England

Please Note

Although every care has been taken with the production of this book to ensure that any projects, designs, modifications and/or programs, etc., contained herewith, operate in a correct and safe manner and also that any components specified are normally available in Great Britain, the Publishers and Author(s) do not accept responsibility in any way for the failure (including fault in design) of any project, design, modification or program to work correctly or to cause damage to any equipment that it may be connected to or used in conjunction with, or in respect of any other damage or injury that may be so caused, nor do the Publishers accept responsibility in any way for the failure to obtain specified components.

Notice is also given that if equipment that is still under warranty is modified in any way or used or connected with home-built equipment then that warranty may be void.

© 1999 BERNARD BABANI (publishing) LTD

First Published - December 1999
Reprinted - November 2000

British Library Cataloguing in Publication Data:

A catalogue record for this book is available from the British Library

ISBN 0 85934 472 X

Cover Design by Gregor Arthur
Printed and Bound in Great Britain by Bath Press

About this Book

Microsoft Word 2000 explained has been written to help users to get to grips with this Microsoft word processor, desk top and Internet publishing package in the fastest possible time. No previous knowledge is assumed, but the book does not describe how to install and use Microsoft Windows. If you need to know more about Windows, then may we suggest you select an appropriate level book for your needs from the 'Books Available' list - the books are loosely graduated in complexity with the less demanding *One step at a time* series, to the more detailed *Explained* series. They are all published by BERNARD BABANI (publishing) Ltd.

The package improves on previous Word capabilities, such as:

- The Office Assistant - the online, natural language interface which assists you with the task in hand.

- Command Bars - the enhanced user interface.

- Multilingual Features - the support for editing and viewing of documents in more than 80 languages.

- Automatic Language Detection - the English (U.S.) version of Word 2000 comes with proofing tools for English, Spanish, and French.

- IntelliSense - the features which help you with your work.

Microsoft Word 2000 is an exciting new package that will help you with the new millennium challenges and opportunities, both personal and business. It offers new tools that use Web technology to provide enhanced workgroup productivity and the ability to access and publish information on the Internet (including the 'effortless' design of your Web site). Unlike previous versions of the package where you had to go through the edit-export-update cycle of Internet or Intranet publishing, Microsoft has made Word 2000 documents browser-readable when you save them as Web pages. Such Web pages are then fully functional Word documents which makes publishing them a live activity.

This book introduces Word with sufficient detail to get you working, then discusses how to share information with other people. No prior knowledge of this package's capabilities is assumed.

The book was written with the busy person in mind. It is not necessary to learn all there is to know about a subject, when reading a few selected pages can usually do the same thing quite adequately. With the help of this book, it is hoped that you will be able to come to terms with Microsoft Word and get the most out of your computer in terms of efficiency, productivity and enjoyment, and that you will be able to do it in the shortest, most effective and informative way.

If you would like to purchase a Companion Disc for any of the listed books by the same author(s), apart from the ones marked with an asterisk, containing the file/program listings which appear in them, then fill in the form at the back of the book and send it to Phil Oliver at the stipulated address.

About the Authors

Noel Kantaris graduated in Electrical Engineering at Bristol University and after spending three years in the Electronics Industry in London, took up a Tutorship in Physics at the University of Queensland. Research interests in Ionospheric Physics, led to the degrees of M.E. in Electronics and Ph.D. in Physics. On return to the UK, he took up a Post-Doctoral Research Fellowship in Radio Physics at the University of Leicester, and then in 1973 a lecturing position in Engineering at the Camborne School of Mines, Cornwall, (part of Exeter University), where between 1978 and 1997 he was also the CSM Computing Manager. At present he is IT Director of FFC Ltd.

Phil Oliver graduated in Mining Engineering at Camborne School of Mines in 1967 and since then has specialised in most aspects of surface mining technology, with a particular emphasis on computer related techniques. He has worked in Guyana, Canada, several Middle Eastern countries, South Africa and the United Kingdom, on such diverse projects as: the planning and management of bauxite, iron, gold and coal mines; rock excavation contracting in the UK; international mining equipment sales and international mine consulting for a major mining house in South Africa. In 1988 he took up a lecturing position at Camborne School of Mines (part of Exeter University) in Surface Mining and Management. He retired from full-time lecturing in 1998, to spend more time writing, consulting and developing Web sites for clients.

Acknowledgements

We would like to thank the staff of Text 100 Limited for providing the software programs on which this work was based. We would also like to thank colleagues at the Camborne School of Mines for the helpful tips and suggestions which assisted us in the writing of this book.

Trademarks

Arial and **Times New Roman** are registered trademarks of The Monotype Corporation plc.

HP and LaserJet are registered trademarks of Hewlett Packard Corporation.

IBM is a registered trademark of International Business Machines, Inc.

Intel is a registered trademark of Intel Corporation.

Microsoft, **MS-DOS**, **Windows**, **Windows NT**, and **Visual Basic**, are either registered trademarks or trademarks of Microsoft Corporation.

PostScript is a registered trademark of Adobe Systems Incorporated.

TrueType is a registered trademark of Apple Corporation.

All other brand and product names used in the book are recognised as trademarks, or registered trademarks, of their respective companies.

Contents

1. Package Overview 1

Hardware and Software Requirements 2
Installing Microsoft Office 2000 3
    Adding or Removing Office Applications 5
Major Word Features 7
    New Features in Word 12
Using the Office Assistant 15
    Customising the Office Assistant 17

2. The Word Environment 19

The Word Screen 20
    The Standard Toolbar 23
    The Formatting Bar 24
    The Status Bar 25
    The Menu Bar Options 26
    Shortcut Menus 31
    Dialogue Boxes 32
The Mouse Pointers 35
Using the Help Menu 37

3. Word Document Basics 41

Entering Text 41
Moving Around a Document 42
Templates and Paragraph Styles 43
    Changing Paragraph Styles 43
Document Screen Displays 44
Changing Default Options 47
    Modifying Margins 47
    Changing the Default Paper Size 47
    Modifying the Paper Source 49
    Modifying the Page Layout 49
    Changing Other Default Options 50
Saving to a File 51
    Selecting File Location 53
    Document Properties 54
    Closing a Document 55
    Opening a Document 56

4. **Editing Word Documents** 57

Adding Buttons to the Standard Toolbar 58
Selecting Text 59
    Copying Blocks of Text 61
    Moving Blocks of Text 62
    Deleting Blocks of Text 62
The Undo Command 63
Finding and Changing Text 63
Page Breaks 66
Using the Spell Checker 67
Using the Thesaurus 68
The Grammar Checker 69
Printing Documents 71

5. **Formatting Word Documents** 75

Formatting Text 75
    Moving Toolbars 77
    Text Enhancements 78
    Paragraph Alignment 79
    Paragraph Spacing 80
    Indenting Text 81
    Inserting Bullets 85
    Inserting Date and Time 86
    Inserting Annotations 87
Formatting with Page Tabs 89
Formatting with Styles 90
    Paragraph Styles 91
Document Templates 93
    Creating a Document Template 93
Special Formatting Features 96
    Changing the Default Character Format 96
    Inserting Special Characters and Symbols 97
    Inserting Other Special Characters 98

6. **Document Enhancements** 99

Page Numbering 99
Using Headers and Footers 101
Using Footnotes 103
Using Multiple Columns on a Page 104

Text Boxes and Frames 105
    Inserting Text Boxes 106
    Moving Text Boxes 107
    Sizing Text Boxes 111
    Rotating Text in a Text Box 112
Importing a Picture 112
    The Picture Bar 114
The Drawing Tools 115
    The Drawing Toolbar 116
    Creating a Drawing 117
    Editing a Drawing 117
    Using Layered Drawings 118
Inserting Objects into a Document 119
    Inserting an Equation 120

7. Using Tables and Graphs 123
Creating a Table 124
    Navigating with the Keyboard 125
    Changing Column Width and Row Height 126
    Entering Expressions 127
    Editing a Table 131
    Formatting a Table 133
Using Microsoft Graph 134
Pre-defined Chart Types 137
    Improving a Microsoft Chart 139

8. Managing Large Documents 141
Outline Mode 141
    Assigning Outline Levels 142
    Outline Buttons 144
    Outline Numbering 145
    Creating a Table of Contents or an Index 146
File Management 148
Assembling a Master Document 151
    Printing a Master Document 152

9. E-mail and Hyperlinks 153

HTML File Format 153
E-mail 155
Word and Outlook 2000 155
    Configuring Outlook for E-mail 155
E-mailing a Document 158
Sending E-mail Messages 159
    The E-mail Header Buttons 162
    Using Signatures 163
    Personalised Stationery 164
Attaching a File 165
The Address Book 166
Using Hypertext Links 167
    Inserting a Hyperlink 167
    Inserting an Internet Hyperlink 168
    Inserting Other Hyperlinks 169
    Drag-and-drop Hyperlinks 170
    Editing Hyperlinks 170

10. Internet Web Pages 171

Creating Web Pages 172
    Using an Existing Word Document 172
    Using the Web Page Wizard 173
    Using a Web Page Template 174
    Adding a Theme to a Page 176
    Adding Movies and Sounds 177
Some HTML Differences 178
Saving Web Pages on the Internet 179
    Web Folders 179
Uploading to an FTP Site 180
    Supporting Files 181

11. Sharing Information 183

Copying or Moving Information 184
    Source File Available without Application 184
    Source File and Application Available 186
Insert an Excel Worksheet in Word 187

Object Linking and Embedding 188
    Embedding a New Object 189
    Linking or Embedding an Existing File 190
    Linking or Embedding Selected Information ... 191
    Editing an Embedded Object 192
Mail Merging Lists 193
    Creating an Address List in Word 196
    Getting an Address List 198

12. Customising Word 2000 201

Word Macro Basics 201
    Recording a Macro 201
    Saving a Macro to Disc 203
    Playing Back a Macro 204
    Attaching Macros/Commands to a Toolbar 205
    Removing Macro or Command Buttons 206
    Editing a Macro 207
    Getting Help with Macros 208
Customising Toolbars and Menus 210
    The Default Toolbars and Menus 210
    Move or Copy Toolbar Buttons 212
    Add or Remove Toolbar Buttons 212
    Create a Custom Toolbar 213
    Manipulating Menu Commands 215
    Restoring Default Toolbars or Menus 216
    Getting Help on Toolbars and Menus 217

13. Glossary of Terms 219

Index 239

1

Package Overview

Microsoft's Word 2000 for Windows 95/98 or higher is a best selling Windows word processor and is fully integrated with all other Microsoft Office 2000 applications. This version of Word, like its predecessor, has particularly strong leanings towards desk top publishing which offers fully editable WYSIWYG (what you see is what you get) modes that can be viewed in various zoom levels, including full page. Couple this with the ability to include and manipulate full colour graphics and you can see the enormous power of the program. You will find using Word 2000 to be both intuitive and easy and you will soon be producing the type of word processed output you would not have dreamt possible.

Word 2000, in common with all other Microsoft Office 2000 applications, makes use of what is known as IntelliSense, which anticipates what you want to do and produces the correct result. For example, AutoCorrect and AutoFormat can, when active, correct common spelling mistakes and format documents automatically. Other Wizards can help you with everyday tasks and/or make complex tasks easier to manage.

Word uses Object Linking and Embedding (OLE) to move and share information seamlessly between Office 2000 applications. For example, you can drag information from one application to another, or you can link information from one application into another. Similarly, Hyperlinks can be used from any of the Office 2000 applications to access other Office documents, files on an internal or external Web or FTP (File Transfer Protocol) site, or HTML (Hypertext Markup Language) files. Hyperlinks help you use your documents with the Internet.

Finally, writing macros in Visual Basic gives you a powerful development platform with which to create custom solutions.

Hardware and Software Requirements

If Microsoft Word 2000 is already installed on your computer, you can safely skip this and the following section of this chapter.

To install and use Word 2000, which comes as part of Microsoft Office 2000, you need an IBM-compatible PC equipped with Intel's Pentium processor. Microsoft suggests a 75 MHz processor for the installation of the Standard edition of Office 2000 which includes Outlook, Word, Excel, and PowerPoint. In addition, you need the following:

- Windows 95/98 (or higher), or Windows NT as the operating system.

- Random access memory (RAM) required is:

   For Windows 9x or higher, 16 MB plus 4 MB for each running application.

   For Windows NT, 32 MB plus 4 MB for each running application.

- Hard disc space required for the Standard edition of Office 2000 is 189 MB.

- CD-ROM drive.

- Video adapter: VGA or higher resolution. If you are embedding colour pictures, you will need a 256-colour video adapter.

- Pointing device: Microsoft Mouse or compatible.

Realistically, to run the above mentioned Office 2000 applications, including Word 2000, with reasonable sized documents, you will need a 100 MHz Pentium PC with at least 32 MB of RAM. To run Microsoft Office 2000 from a network, you must also have a network compatible with your Windows operating environment, such as Microsoft's Windows 95/98 or higher, Windows NT, LAN Manager, etc.

Finally, if you are connected to the Internet, you can take advantage of Word's advanced editing and formatting features when working with e-mail messages. To use Word as your e-mail editor, you must have Microsoft Outlook or Microsoft Exchange installed on your computer and in that program have Word 2000 selected as your e-mail editor.

Installing Microsoft Office 2000

Installing Office 2000 on your computer's hard disc is made very easy using the SETUP program, which even configures it automatically to take advantage of the computer's hardware. One of SETUP's functions is to convert compressed Office files from the CD-ROM, prior to copying them onto your hard disc.

Note: If you are using a virus detection utility, disable it before running SETUP, as it might conflict with it.

To install Microsoft Office, place the distribution CD in your CD drive and close it. The auto-start program on the CD will start the SETUP program automatically. If that does not work, click the **Start** button, and select the **Run** command which opens the Run dialogue box, shown below.

Next, type in the **Open** box:

```
G:\setup
```

as shown here.

In our case we used the CD-ROM in the G: drive; yours could be different. Clicking the **OK** button,

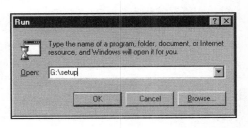

starts the installation of Microsoft Office 2000. SETUP displays the first of several screens.

We suggest that you follow the instructions displayed on the screen. SETUP goes through the following procedure:

- Prompts you to type your name and the name of your organisation (optional).

- Prompts you to type in the Product Key.

- Asks you to accept the licence agreement.

- Prompts you to supply the path to the directory where you want to install Word, and then checks your system and the available hard disc space.

- Searches your system's discs for other installed Office components and asks you whether an older version of Word should be removed or not.

Follow the SETUP instructions on the screen, until the istallation of Microsoft Office program files is completed. The SETUP program will modify your system files automatically so that you can start Word easily by creating and displaying a new entry in the **Start, Programs** cascade menu. During installation, the Office Shortcut Bar is collated and added to the Windows Start Up program so that it will be displayed automatically on your screen whenever you start your PC.

In addition, Office 2000 adds to the **Start** menu the two entries shown at the top of the adjacent screen dump; the **New Office Document**, and the **Open Office Document**. The first allows you to select in a displayed dialogue box the tab containing the type of document you want to work with, such as letters & faxes, memos, or presentations, to mention but a few. Double-clicking the type of document or template you want, automatically loads the appropriate application. The second entry allows you to work with existing documents. Opening a document, first starts the application originally used to create it, then opens the document.

Adding or Removing Office Applications

To add or remove an Office application, left-click the **Start** button at the bottom left corner of the screen, point to **Settings**, then click the **Control Panel** option on the Windows pop-up menu, as shown below.

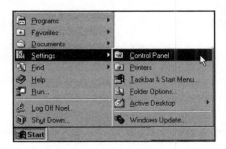

This opens the Control Panel dialogue box. Next, double-click the Add/Remove Programs icon, shown here to the left, to open the dialogue box below. Click the Install/Uninstall tab and select the Microsoft Office 2000 program, and then click the **Add/Remove** button.

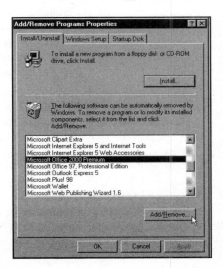

This requires you insert the Office 2000 CD into your CD drive, which causes SETUP to display the following Maintenance Mode dialogue box:

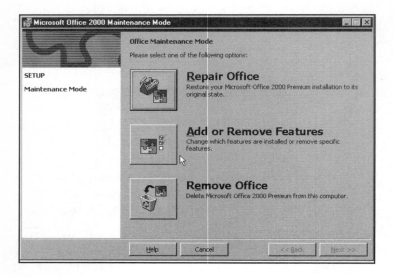

Selecting the **Add or Remove Features** opens up the dialogue box to the left in which you can select which Office applications and features you want installed.

Note the additional buttons on the above screen. Use the **Repair Office** button to reinstall the whole of Office 2000, or to find and fix any errors in your original installation. Finally, you can use the **Remove Office** button to uninstall all of the Office 2000 applications.

Major Word Features

Some of the major features Microsoft Word 2000 contains, include the ability to:

- Employ the Office Assistant which uses IntelliSense natural-language technology. It anticipates the kind of help you need and suggests Help topics appropriate to the work you are doing at the time. Further, you can have the Assistant offer to start a Wizard when you start certain tasks, such as creating a letter.

- Drag and drop when editing text, tables, and graphics in a document and across windows - this is more convenient than cutting and pasting.

- Use shortcut menus relevant to the type of work you are carrying out at the time, to help speed your work.

- Create documents that have different formatting, multiple columns, and a variety of page layouts.

- Add comments and annotations to a document without changing the original text.

- Create a glossary of text and graphics which can be inserted in any part of a document.

- Insert footnotes in any part of a document's page with automatic numbering.

- AutoCorrect which fixes common typing errors as you work, and AutoText which speeds up the insertion of frequently used text, tables, lists, and graphics, into your document.

- Correct your spelling with an extensive spell checker - you can even add special words to it.

- Check a document's grammar and style and customise the latter to suit your needs.

- Look up the meaning of words and find synonyms using the thesaurus.

- Create tables in a document automatically, which can contain text, numbers, pictures and objects - formatting can be applied to the whole, or individual parts.

- Use the Draw Table tool which allows you to create and customise tables in a similar way to using a pen and paper.

- Use the Eraser tool which allows you to easily remove any cell, row, or column partition to merge two adjacent cells in a table.

- Use a set of drawing and graphics tools in Office Art, which gives you all the flexibility required for manipulating pictures.

- Add pictures created in another application to a document, scale them proportionally, or crop them to your requirements.

- Wrap text around irregular objects of any shape or size, and the ability to rotate text in a table cell so that it appears vertical.

- Create objects, such as graphs, charts and equations, which can be modified, edited, moved and/or copied.

- Insert a frame around a paragraph, picture or object, then move the frame and its contents, or change its size.

- Use the Bullets and Numbering command which can easily add bullets and numbers to multiple-level lists.

- Use the Heading Numbering command which can create numbered headings with built-in heading styles.

- Use AutoCaption which helps you to quickly add captions and create cross-references to captions, headings, tables, and other items.

- View documents in a variety of ways, preview a document before printing, print a document or print/view information about a document.

- Maximise the text area on your screen by hiding menus, toolbars, and rulers.

- Use automated printing of envelopes, provided the printer's envelope feeder has been installed.

- Transparently import existing files produced by most versions of Microsoft and WordPerfect word processors, as well as worksheets and databases produced in Excel, Lotus 1-2-3, and dBase formats.

- Link and embed information or objects (OLE) created in other Windows applications into a Word document.

- Use the optional user's help to ease the changeover from WordPerfect to Word.

- Network the program so users can share information.

- Automatically format a document as you type. Typing three or more consecutive hyphens (-) and pressing <Enter> creates a thin line border, while typing three or more consecutive equal signs (=) and pressing <Enter> creates a double-line border.

- Automatically apply a built-in heading style to text as you type. Typing a line of text and pressing <Enter> twice, causes Word to apply Heading 1 style to the text, while starting a line with a tab, results in Heading 2 style.

- Automatically change ordinary numbers and fractions you type in to make them easier to read, as shown here.

You type	Word changes the format to
1st	1st
2nd	2nd
1/2	$\frac{1}{2}$

- Automatically create numbered or bulleted lists. For example, starting a list with a number (or letter) followed by a period (.), causes Word to insert a number (or letter) bullet in front of each line in the list. Typing an asterisk followed by a space or tab, results in a bulleted list similar to the ones we are using here.

- Automatically correct text and replace a number of key presses with particular symbols, as shown to the right.

You type	Word inserts
:)	☺
:(	☹
<--	←
-->	→
<==	⇐
==>	⇒
<=>	⇔
(c)	©
(TM)	TM

- Open or find documents by simply clicking the **Open** option on the **File** menu.

- See the contents of documents without opening them. To preview a document, select it, click the View button and choose the Preview option.

- Manage your files from within the Open dialogue box. Right-clicking a document opens a shortcut menu, shown here, to help you with appropriate house-keeping functions.

- Check your spelling while you type. If a word is not in the dictionary, Word marks it with a wavy red line. To select from a list of spelling choices, right-click the marked word.

- Choose from three built-in families of templates; contemporary, elegant, and professional. Choosing one of these, can help you create a consistent look for your document.

- Mark text with a highlighter, so that it is easier to emphasise important parts of a message. To mark text, select it and click the Highlight button, shown here, and select the colour you want to use from the displayed list.

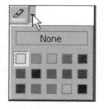

- Use the AutoSummarize feature which can analyse your document statistically and linguistically to provide a summary of the key points in it.

- Use the Letter Wizard dialogue box which allows you to choose letter elements to make it easy to build your letter. Word can remember to whom you have sent a letter and stores all related information, such as addresses, etc., in a list. To send a letter to a previous recipient, all you have to do is select the name of the person from a list, and Word automatically fills in the rest of the information.

- Use the natural-language Grammar Checker which flags mistakes and provides you with effective suggestions.

- Employ an extensive set of features applicable to the Web, including the use of Hyperlinks which are used to link to any Microsoft Office, HTML, or other file on any internal or external Web site or file server. Clicking a Hyperlink causes a jump to its destination.

- Design a Web page with the help of the Web Page Wizard which provides customised Web templates that you can easily modify to your needs - you can add pictures and music to a Web page as well as to a Word document.

- Integrate seamlessly with Exchange and Outlook to use Word as your standard e-mail editor.

- Maintain a working history of a document by using the Versioning feature. This allows you to see exactly who did what to a document and when. All Versioning information is kept with the document, so that you don't have to store and track multiple copies of a document.

- Use revision marks so that intended changes can be seen easily - such changes can then be accepted or rejected by another user.

- Consolidate all changes and comments from different reviewers of a given document. Reviewers can modify separate copies of the same document, but you can merge all their comments and changes into the original in one easy step.

New Features in Word

Word 2000 has many new features over and above those found in previous versions of the program. These include:

- The use of the AutoCorrect exceptions list to prevent unwanted spelling corrections.

- The ability to maintain a separate list of AutoCorrect entries for each language used. Word will switch to the appropriate list based on the language formatting in the document.

- The use of the Click and Type facility to quickly insert text, graphics, tables, or other items by double-clicking in a blank area of a document when in a Web or Print Layout View.

- The use of the new Office Clipboard to collect objects from all of your programs, including your Web browser, and paste them where and when you need them. You can store up to 12 objects on the Office Clipboard.

- The ability to check the spelling and grammar of text in another language, provided you have installed the spelling and grammar tools for that language. If the selected language is then enabled in Word for editing, it will be automatically detected in your documents and the correct spelling and grammar tools will be used.

- The ability to hyphenate documents correctly in the language being used at the time.

- The ability to create nested tables - tables inside other tables. You can click and drag to draw a nested table just as you would any table.

- The ability to adjust any row's height directly in a table by dragging the row border up or down, just as you adjust column widths.

- The ability to change the size of the entire table while maintaining the same row and column proportions.

- The use of the mouse to move your table to another position on the page.

- The ability to align text both vertically and horizontally from convenient alignment toolbar buttons. If your text is oriented vertically, the buttons automatically adjust to give you the correct alignment.

- The use of the Web Folders feature to manage your files stored on a Web server. You can access Web Folders through Windows Explorer or through any Microsoft Office program.

- The use of a wizard which provides customised Web templates that you can easily modify to meet your needs.

- The use of frames to create an organised Web site that allows you to communicate more information to your audience.

- The ability to use a Web Layout View, without leaving Word, to see how your Web pages will look in a Web browser.

- The use of built-in themes which contain unified design elements and colour schemes for background images, bullets, fonts, horizontal lines, and other document elements to create consistent-looking Web pages.

- The ability to add a picture to a Web page, just as you do with a Word document. Such objects can be edited even after you save your document as a Web page.

- The provision of a built-in set of colourful graphical images which can be used as bullets on Web pages to make information more noticeable.

- The extension of the built-in borders and shading functionality in Word to provide Web-specific colourful horizontal lines that can be included on Web pages.

- WYSIWYG (what you see is what you get) support for authoring Web pages with commonly used tags, such as tables, fonts, and background sound.

- The ability to create scripts and HTML-based client solutions within any Office program by using the Visual Studio development environment. There is full browser support for debugging, and script anchors can be used in Office documents.

- The ability to e-mail a copy of a document directly from Microsoft Word. In effect, the document is the e-mail message so you can edit it directly, without having to open or save an attachment. Messages from Word are in HTML format, so your recipients won't require special software to view the message.

Most of these new and old features of Word 2000 will be examined in the following chapters of this book. Whenever possible, we introduce practical examples that you are encouraged to type in and use to illustrate particular points, and then save on disc for future use.

Using the Office Assistant

The Office Assistant is a central source of application information. No matter which Office 2000 application you are using, the Assistant is there to help you.

To find out how it works, start one of the Office applications (we have used Word), then click the relevant Office Assistant button, shown here, with

the left mouse button, type the word **help** in the displayed 'What would you like to do?' box, shown to the left, and left-click the **S**earch button.

A list of help topics is then displayed, as shown to the right. To see more topics, left-click the small triangle at the bottom of the list with the caption 'See more', to display additional topics, as shown below.

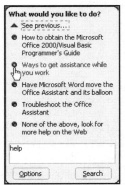

To find out how you can use the Office Assistant, click the 'Ways to get assistance while you work' option which causes the display of the screen shown on the next page. From this latter screen you can find out all there is to know about the Office Assistant.

The very same screen can be displayed from all Office applications, with only the title of the window and the 'Finding out what's new in ...' hypertext link, changing to reflect the application in use.

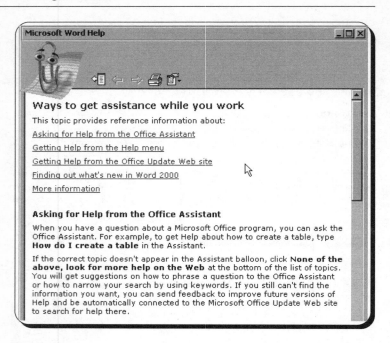

Note the Web browser type buttons at the top of the screen. These allow you to carry out the following functions:

⊲▤	**Show** - click this button to display the help screen tabs which allow you to access Help's Contents, Answer Wizard, and Index.
⇐	**Back** - if more than one help screen has been opened, click this button to go back to the previously opened help screen.
⇨	**Forward** - if you have moved back to a previous help screen, click this button to move forward through opened help screens.
🖨	**Print** - click this button to print the contents of the current help screen.
🖹▾	**Options** - click this button to open up a menu of options which control all of the above facilities plus the ability to select the Internet Options dialogue box.

Customising the Office Assistant

You can customise the Office Assistant to a great degree. Not only can you change the way it responds to your enquiries, but you can also switch it off once you have mastered a particular Office application.

To see the default options settings of the Office Assistant, activate it, left-click on it, and left-click the **Options** button on the displayed box, shown here.

Doing this, causes the following dialogue box to be displayed on your screen:

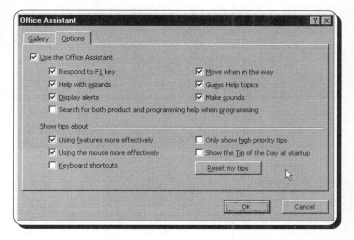

As you can see, it is possible to choose from several options. To change the shape of your Office Assistant (there are eight shapes to choose from - see next page), either left-click the Gallery tab of the above dialogue box, or right-click the Office Assistant and select the **Choose Assistant** option from the displayed menu, as shown here.

Either action displays the following dialogue box in which you can select your preferred Assistant shape by left-clicking the **Next** button.

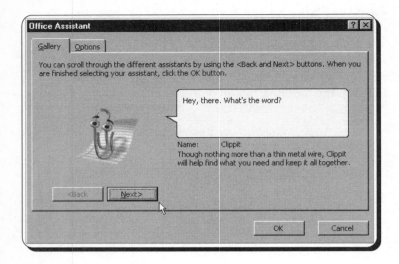

The shapes of the available Assistants are as follows:

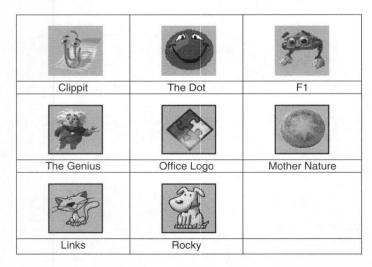

Clippit	The Dot	F1
The Genius	Office Logo	Mother Nature
Links	Rocky	

2

The Word Environment

Word is started in Windows either by clicking the **Start** button then selecting **Programs** and clicking on the 'Microsoft Word' icon on the cascade menu, clicking the Word icon, or the 'Open Office Document' icon on the Office Shortcut Bar, or by clicking and double-clicking on a Word document file. In the latter case the document will be loaded into Word at the same time.

If you have used a previous version of Word it might be a good idea to use **The Office Assistant** and search for *what's new*. Selecting the 'What's new in Microsoft Word 2000?' option (pointed to below), displays a further list of options which you might like to view.

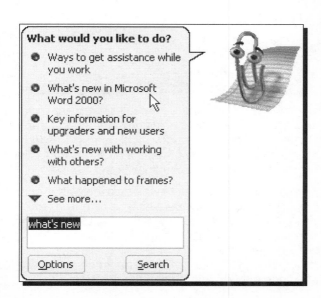

The Word Screen

The opening 'blank' screen of Word 2000 is shown below. It is perhaps worth spending some time looking at the various parts that make up this screen. Word follows the usual Microsoft Windows conventions and if you are familiar with these you can skip through this section. Otherwise a few minutes might be well spent here.

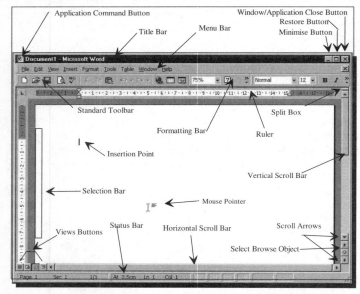

The window as shown takes up the full screen area available. If you click on the application restore button, you can make Word show in a smaller window. This can be useful when you are running several applications at the same time and you want to transfer between them with the mouse.

Note that in this case, the Word window displays an empty document with the title 'Document1', and has a solid 'Title bar', indicating that it is the active application window. Although multiple windows can be displayed simultaneously, you can only enter data into the active window (which will always be displayed on top). Title bars of non active windows appear a lighter shade than that of the active one.

The Word screen is divided into several areas which have the following functions:

Area	*Function*
Command buttons	Clicking on the command button, (see upper-left corner of the Word window), displays a pull-down menu which can be used to control the program window. It allows you to restore, move, size, minimise, maximise, and close the window.
Title Bar	The bar at the top of a window which displays the application name and the name of the current document.
Minimise Button	When clicked on, this button minimises a document or the application to an icon on the Windows Taskbar.
Restore Button	When clicked on, this button restores the active window to the position and size that was occupied before it was maximised. The restore button is then replaced by a Maximise button, as shown here, which is used to set the window to full screen size.
Close button	The extreme top right button that you click to close a window.
Menu Bar	The bar below the Title bar which allows you to choose from several menu options.

Clicking on a menu item displays the pull-down menu associated with that item.

Standard Toolbar

The bar below the Menu bar which contains buttons that give you mouse click access to the functions most often used in the program. These are grouped according to function.

Formatting Bar

The buttons on the Formatting Bar allow you to change the attributes of a font, such as italic and underline, and also to format text in various ways. The Formatting Bar contains three boxes; a style box, a font box and a size box which show which style, font and size of characters are currently being used. These boxes give access to other installed styles, fonts and character sizes.

Ruler

The area where you can see and set tabulation points and indents.

Split Box

The area above the top vertical scroll button which when dragged allows you to split the screen.

Scroll Bars

The areas on the screen that contain scroll boxes in vertical and horizontal bars. Clicking on these bars allows you to control the part of a document which is visible on the screen.

Scroll Arrows

The arrowheads at each end of each scroll bar at which you can click to scroll the screen up and down one line, or left and right 10% of the screen, at a time.

Selection Bar	The area on the screen in the left margin of the Word window (marked here with a box for convenience), where the mouse pointer changes to an arrow that slants to the right. Clicking the left mouse button once selects the current line, while clicking twice selects the current paragraph.
Insertion pointer	The pointer used to specify the place of text insertion.
Views Buttons	Clicking these buttons changes screen views quickly.
Status Bar	The bottom line of the document window that displays status information.

The Standard Toolbar

This is located below the Menu bar at the top of the Word screen and contains command buttons. To action a command, left-click its button with the mouse. Not only can you control what buttons show on the various toolbars, but as you work with Word the buttons you use most often are displayed on them automatically.

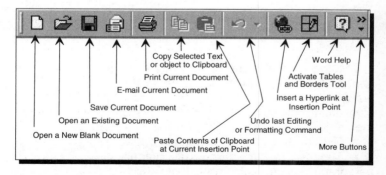

Copy Selected Text or object to Clipboard
Word Help
Print Current Document
Activate Tables and Borders Tool
E-mail Current Document
Insert a Hyperlink at Insertion Point
Save Current Document
Undo last Editing or Formatting Command
Open an Existing Document
Open a New Blank Document
Paste Contents of Clipboard at Current Insertion Point
More Buttons

The use of these Standard Toolbar buttons will be discussed in great detail, with worked examples, in the next chapter.

The Formatting Bar

This is located to the right of or below the Standard Toolbar, and is divided into sections that contain command buttons, as shown below.

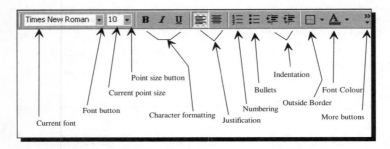

The Current font box shows the current typeface. Clicking on the down-arrow button to the right of it allows you to change the typeface of any selected text. The Current point size box shows the size of selected characters which can be changed by clicking on the down-arrow button next to it and selecting another size from the displayed list.

Next, are three character formatting buttons which allow you to enhance selected text by emboldening, italicising, or underlining it. The next two buttons allow you to change the justification of a selected paragraph, and the next four help you set the different types of Numbering and Indentation options. The last two buttons allow you to add an Outside Border to selected text or objects, and change the font colour of selected text.

Clicking on the More Buttons area, opens up the menu shown here with additional options for justifying selected paragraphs and highlighting text. The first option displays the name of the current style (Normal) in a box. Clicking the down-arrow against this box, opens up a menu of default paragraph styles with their font sizes.

Once the Style box is opened, from then on, it appears to the left of the Font box, replacing other formatting icons.

The Status Bar

This is located at the bottom of the Word window and is used to display statistics about the active document.

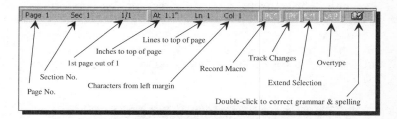

For example, when a document is being opened, the Status bar displays for a short time its name and length in terms of total number of characters. Once a document is opened, the Status bar displays the statistics of the document at the insertion point; here it is on Page 1, Section 1, 1 character from the left margin.

Double-clicking the left of the status bar displays the Find and Replace dialogue box, as shown below.

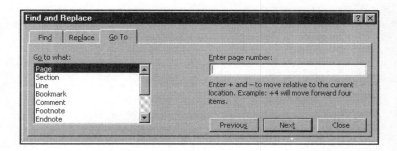

This is shown with the **Go To** tab selected. You can choose which page, section line, etc., of the document to go to, or you can use the other tabs to **Find** and **Replace** text (more about this later).

Double-clicking the other features on the Status bar will activate these features.

The Menu Bar Options

Each menu bar option has associated with it a pull-down sub-menu. To activate the menu, either press the <Alt> key, which causes the first option of the menu (in this case the **File** menu option) to be selected, then use the right and left arrow keys to highlight any of the options in the menu, or use the mouse to point to an option. Pressing either the <Enter> key, or the left mouse button, reveals the pull-down sub-menu of the highlighted menu option. The sub-menu of the **File** option is shown below.

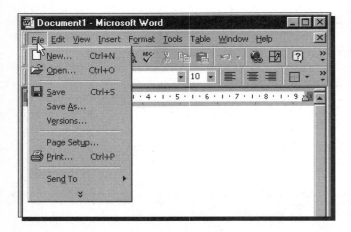

Note that in this version of Word, the drop-down sub-menu displays only the most important options, but you have the option to view the full sub-menu by highlighting the double arrow-heads at the bottom of it, by either pointing to that part of the sub-menu with the mouse or using the down-arrow cursor key to move the highlighted bar down.

The full sub-menu of the **File** menu option is displayed on the next page. However, the order of the sub-menu options in both the short and the full version of the sub-menu could differ from ours. This is because Word, and the other Office 2000 applications, now learn from your actions and automatically promote the items you choose from menu extensions on to the shortened version of the sub-menu.

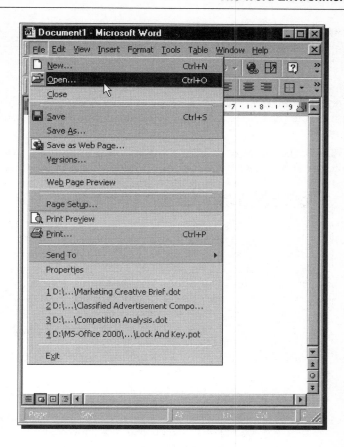

Menu options can also be activated directly by pressing the
<Alt> key followed by the underlined letter of the required
option. Thus, pressing <Alt+F>, causes the pull-down **File**
sub-menu to be displayed. You can use the up and down
arrow keys to move the highlighted bar up and down a
sub-menu, or the right and left arrow keys to move along the
options in the menu bar. Pressing the <Enter> key selects
the highlighted option or executes the highlighted command.
Pressing the <Esc> key once, closes the pull-down
sub-menu, while pressing the <Esc> key for a second time,
closes the menu system.

Some of the sub-menu options can be accessed with 'quick key' combinations from the keyboard. Such combinations are shown on the drop-down menus, for example, <Ctrl+S> is the quick key for the **Save** option in the **File** sub-menu. If a sub-menu option is not available, at any time, it will display in a grey colour. Some menu options only appear in Word when that tool is being used, but the ones described below remain constant.

The following is a brief description of the standard menu options. For a more detailed description of each sub-menu item, use the on-line **Help** system (to be described shortly).

File Produces a pull-down menu of mainly file related tasks, such as creating a **New** document, the ability to **Open**, or **Close** files, and **Save** files with the same name, or **Save As** a different name, or even **Save as Web Page**. You can use **Page Setup** to set the margins and the size of your printed page, **Print Preview** a document on screen before committing it to paper, **Print** a document and select your current printer. You can view a specific file's **Properties**, and direct documents to other users who share resources with you, using the **Send To** option. Finally, you can **Exit** the program. Above this last sub-menu option, Word also displays the last four documents you used so that you can open them easily.

Edit Produces a pull-down menu which allows you to **Undo** changes made, **Cut**, **Copy** and **Paste** text and graphics, **Find** specific text in a document, **Find and Replace** text, jump to any location in a document, view and update **Links**, or open a selected **Object**.

View Produces a pull-down menu which contains screen display options which allow you to change the editing view to **Normal**, **Web Layout**, **Print Layout** or **Outline**.

You can further control whether to display the **Toolbars**, or the **Ruler**, show a list of **Headers/Footers**, open windows for viewing **Footnotes**, or **Comments**, display a **Full Screen** and determine the scale of the editing view by using the **Zoom** option.

Insert   Produces a pull-down menu which allows you to insert **Breaks** to the ends of pages, columns, or sections, add **Page Numbers** to a document, or insert the **Date and Time** into a document. You can also insert or define **AutoText** items of frequently used text or graphics, insert a **Field** (instruction) for computed contents, or insert special characters with **Symbol**. Further, you can insert a note and activate the **Comment** pane, insert a **Footnote** reference, place a **Caption** above or below a selected object, or a **Cross-reference**. The **Index and Tables** option allows you to build an index entry, an index, or table of contents, tables, etc. Finally, you can insert a **Picture**, a **Text Box**, the contents of a **File**, or an **Object** into the active document and assign a name (**Bookmark**) to a section of your document, or insert **Hyperlinks** to other documents.

Format   Produces a pull-down menu which allows you to alter the appearance of text, both on the screen and when printed. Such features as **Font**, size, colour, alignment, print spacing, justification, and enhancements (bold, underlined and italic) are included. You can change the indent and spacing of a selected **Paragraph**, create bullet or number lists and change the numbering options for heading level styles, change the **Border and Shading** of a selected paragraph, table cell(s), or picture, or change the **Columns** format of the selected section.

You can also set and clear **Tabs**, format the first character of a paragraph as a **Drop Cap**(ital), change **Text Direction**, and **Change Case**. You can further set the **Background** colour, add a **Theme**, a **Frame**, select options to **AutoFormat** a document, browse and apply or modify **Styles**, or change the fill, line, size and position of a selected **Object**.

Tools

Produces a pull-down menu that gives access to the **Spelling and Grammar** checker, use the **Language** option to change the **Language** formatting of the selected characters, or activate the **Thesaurus** and **Hyphenation** options. You can also display the **Word Count** statistics of the current document, and add or delete **AutoCorrect** entries.

You can further **Track Changes** to a document, **Merge** and **Protect** documents, activate **Online Collaboration**, prepare for **Mail Merge**, or create and print **Envelopes and Labels**. Finally, you can run, create, delete or edit a **Macro** (a set of instructions), **Customize** Word to your requirements and change various Word **Options**.

Table

You can use the **Draw Table** or **Insert Table** option of the pull-down menu to create a table of specified rows and columns at the insertion point. Once a table exists, the majority of the options of the pull-down menu become available to you. From here you can **Insert Rows**, **Delete**, **Merge** and **Split Cells**, **Select** a **Row**, a **Column** or a **Table**, or insert a paragraph mark above the current table row by using the **Split Table** option.

Further, you can select the **Table AutoFormat** option to choose from a set of pre-formatted table styles and have them applied to your table, change the **Cell Height and Width**, and toggle the table **Headings** attribute on and off. Finally, you can select a section of text and use the **Convert Text to Table** option to have it incorporated within a table, rearrange a selection into a specified **Sort** order, insert a **Formula** in a cell, and toggle the table **Gridlines** on and off.

<u>W</u>indow   Produces a menu to open a **New Window**, and control the display of existing open windows on the screen.

<u>H</u>elp   Activates the help menu which you can use to access the **Microsoft Word Help**, **Hide the Office Assistant**, the **What's This** facility, or the **Office on the Web** option (if you are connected to the Internet). You can also get help if you are a **WordPerfect** user, **Detect and Repair** errors in Word, or use the **About Microsoft World** option to open up a dialogue box from which you can find out information about your system, or get information on Technical Support.

Shortcut Menus

New to this and the three previous versions of Word are context-sensitive shortcut menus. If you click the right mouse button on any screen, or document, a shortcut menu is displayed with the most frequently used commands relating to the type of work you were doing at the time.

The composite screen dump on the next page shows in turn the shortcut menus that open when the editing area is selected, a table is selected, or either of the Toolbars is selected. In the first shortcut menu the **Cut** and **Copy** commands only become effective if you select part of a sentence before right-clicking (more about this later).

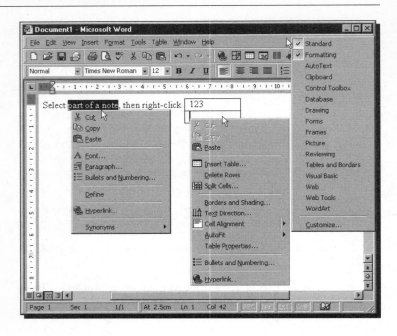

So, whatever you are doing in Word, you have rapid access to a menu of relevant functions by right-clicking your mouse. Left-clicking the mouse at a menu selection will choose that function, while right-clicking on an area outside the shortcut menu (or pressing the <Esc> key), closes down the shortcut menu.

Dialogue Boxes

Three periods after a sub-menu option or command, means that a dialogue box will open when the option or command is selected. A dialogue box is used for the insertion of additional information, such as the name of a file or path.

To see a dialogue box, press <Alt+F>, and select the **Open** option. The 'Open' dialogue box is displayed, as shown on the next page.

When a dialogue box opens, the easiest way to move around it is by clicking with the mouse, otherwise the <Tab> key can be used to move the cursor from one column in the box to another (<Shift+Tab> moves the cursor backwards). Alternatively you can move directly to a desired field by holding the <Alt> key down and pressing the underlined letter in the field name.

Within a column of options you must use the arrow keys to move from one to another. Having selected an option or typed in information, you must press a command button such as the **Open** or **Cancel** button, or choose from additional options.

To select the **Open** button with the mouse, simply point and click, while with the keyboard you must first press the <Tab> key until the dotted rectangle, or focus, moves to the required button, and then press the <Enter> key. Pressing <Enter> at any time while a dialogue box is open, will cause the marked items to be selected and the box to be closed.

Some dialogue boxes contain List boxes which show a column of available choices, similar to the one at the top of the previous screen dump which appears by pressing the down-arrow button, as shown overleaf.

If there are more choices than can be seen in the area

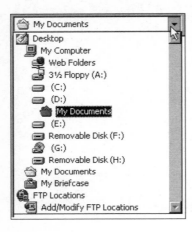

provided, use the scroll bars to reveal them. To select a single item from a List box, either double-click the item, or use the arrow keys to highlight the item and press <Enter>.

Other dialogue boxes contain Option buttons with a list of mutually exclusive items, as shown below.

The default choice is marked with a black dot against its name, while unavailable options are dimmed. To see the above option buttons, use the **File, New** command to open the New dialogue box.

Other dialogue boxes contain Check boxes, like the one below, which offer a list of options you can switch on or off.

Selected options show a tick in the box against the option name, while incompatible options appear greyed out. If you want to see the adjacent Check boxes, use the **Edit, Find** command to open the Find and Replace dialogue box.

To cancel a dialogue box, either click the **Cancel** button, or press the <Esc> key. Pressing the <Esc> key in succession, closes one dialogue box at a time, and eventually aborts the menu option.

The Mouse Pointers

In Microsoft Word, as with all other graphical based programs, using a mouse makes many operations both easier and more fun to carry out.

Word 2000 makes use of the mouse pointers available in Windows, some of the most common of which are illustrated below. When Word is initially started up the first you will see is the hourglass, which turns into an upward pointing hollow arrow once the individual application screen appears on your display. Other shapes depend on the type of work you are doing at the time.

 The hourglass which displays when you are waiting while performing a function.

 The arrow which appears when the pointer is placed over menus, scrolling bars, and buttons.

 The I-beam which appears in normal text areas of the screen. For additional 'Click and Type' pointer shapes, see the table overleaf.

 The 4-headed arrow which appears when you choose to move a table, a chart area, or a frame.

 The double arrows which appear when over the border of a window, used to drag the side and alter the size of the window.

 The Help hand which appears in the Help windows, and is used to access 'hypertext' type links.

Word 2000, like other Windows packages, has additional mouse pointers which facilitate the execution of selected commands. Some of these, shown on the next page, have the following functions:

↓   The vertical pointer which appears when pointing over a column in a table or worksheet and used to select the column.

➡   The horizontal pointer which appears when pointing at a row in a table or worksheet and used to select the row.

⇗   The slanted arrow which appears when the pointer is placed in the selection bar area of text or a table.

◄‖►   The vertical split arrow which appears when pointing over the area separating two columns and used to size a column.

≑   The horizontal split arrow which appears when pointing over the area separating two rows and used to size a row.

+   The cross which you drag to extend or fill a series.

⫽   The draw pointer which appears when you are drawing freehand.

Word 2000 introduces the following Click and Type pointer shapes which appear as you move the I-beam pointer into a specific formatting zone; their shape indicating which formatting will apply when you double-click.

I≡	Align left	≡I	Align right
I≣	Centre	I≜	Left indent
I≡⊡	Left text wrap	⊡≣I	Right text wrap

If you don't see the Click and Type pointer shape, activate the facility using the **Tools**, **Options** command, then click the Edit tab and check the **Enable click and type** box.

Word has a few additional mouse pointers to the ones above, but their shapes are mostly self-evident.

Using the Help Menu

Another way of getting help in
Word (apart from using the Office
Assistant), is to use the **F1**
function key to get directly to the
Context and Index help screens.
To do so, however, you will first
have to switch off the Office
Assistant by right-clicking it and
selecting **Options** from the
drop-down menu. This opens the following dialogue box, in
which you must clear the box against **Use the Office
Assistant**, as shown below.

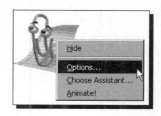

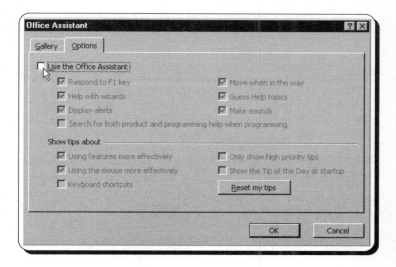

Next time you press the **F1** function key, the Office Help
screen appears as shown on the next page. You can either
view information on the screen or print it on paper.
Left-clicking the Index tab, displays a dialogue box with three
areas for typing, selecting and displaying information, as
shown.

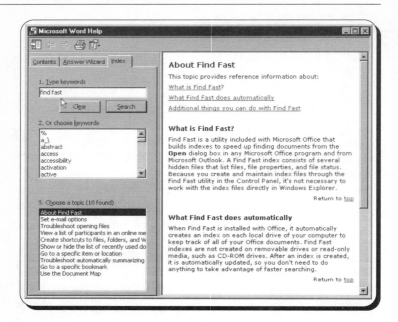

Typing, for example, the words ***find fast*** in the first 'Type keywords' box, causes a list of related topics to appear automatically in the second 'Or choose key words' box. Selecting one or more matching words from the displayed list narrows down the selection of topics appearing in the third 'Choose a topic' box. Finally, selecting a topic from the third display box by left-clicking it, displays information on your selection.

If the keyword you want to choose is not visible within the display area of the second box, use the scroll bar to get to it.

As an exercise, click the Answer Wizard tab of the Help dialogue box and type the words 'backward compatibility' in the 'What would you like to do' box and click the **S̲earch** button. Immediately the topic 'Results of saving Word 2000 documents in other formats' appears highlighted at the top of the list in the second text box, as shown on the next page. As each topic in this list is selected, information about it is automatically displayed in the adjacent text box.

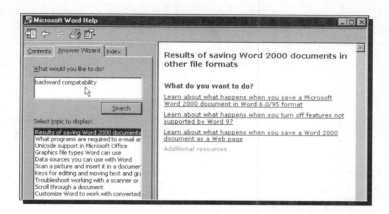

Next, left-click the first item to display all you need to know, in this instance, about the Word 2000, 95, and 6.0 file formats. Similar searches carried out from other Office 2000 applications will reveal what you should do if you require backward compatibility.

It is worth while exploring the different ways in which you can get help with or without the Office Assistant. For

example, another way of getting context sensitive help is to select the '**What's This?**' option from the extended **Help** sub-menu, then move the modified mouse pointer to an area of the document, or onto a particular Toolbar

button, or menu item, and press the left mouse button.

Finally, click the Contents tab of the Help screen to open up an impressive list of topics relating to the Word 2000 program. Left-clicking a selected book, displays the topics and other books it might contain. As each topic is selected, information about that topic appears on the adjacent screen, as shown overleaf.

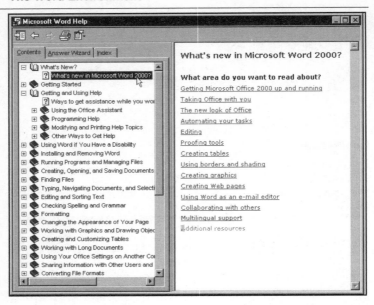

Note the small '+' signs to the left of each book. Left-clicking this sign, opens up the relevant book, indicated by a '-' sign. Do spend some time here to learn, particularly what is new in Word. Other topics can always be explored later.

3

Word Document Basics

When the program is first used, all Word's features default to those shown on page 20 (apart from showing the ruler). It is quite possible to use Word in this mode, without changing any main settings, but obviously it is possible to customise the package to your needs, as we shall see later.

Entering Text

In order to illustrate some of Word's capabilities, you need to have a short text at hand. We suggest you type the memo below into a new document. At this stage, don't worry if the length of the lines below differ from those on your display.

As you type in text, any time you want to force a new line, or paragraph, just press <Enter>. While typing within a paragraph, Word sorts out line lengths automatically (known as 'word wrap'), without you having to press any keys to move to a new line.

MEMO TO PC USERS
Networked Computers
The microcomputers in the Data Processing room are a mixture of IBM compatible PCs with Pentium processors running at various speeds. They all have 3.5" floppy drives of 1.44MB capacity, and most also have CD-ROM drives. The PCs are connected to various printers via a network; the Laser printers available giving best output.

The computer you are using will have at least a 3.0GB capacity hard disc on which a number of software programs, including the latest version of Windows, have been installed. To make life easier, the hard disc is highly structured with each program installed in a separate folder (directory).

Moving Around a Document

You can move the cursor around a document with the normal direction keys, and with the key combinations listed below.

To move	*Press*
Left one character	←
Right one character	→
Up one line	↑
Down one line	↓
Left one word	Ctrl+←
Right one word	Ctrl+→
To beginning of line	Home
To end of line	End
To paragraph beginning	Ctrl+↑
To paragraph end	Ctrl+↓
Up one screen	PgUp
Down one screen	PgDn
To top of previous page	Ctrl+PgUp
To top of next page	Ctrl+PgDn
To beginning of file	Ctrl+Home
To end of file	Ctrl+End

To jump to a specified page number in a multi-page document, either double-click the left of the status bar to display the Find and Replace dialogue box, then click the Go To tab, or use the **Edit**, **Go To** command (or <Ctrl+G>), shown here and to be explained shortly.

Obviously, you need to become familiar with the above methods of moving the cursor around a document, particularly if you are not using a mouse and you spot an error in a document which needs to be corrected, which is the subject of the latter half of this chapter.

Templates and Paragraph Styles

As we saw under the Formatting Bar section earlier, when you start Word for the first time, the Style box contains the word **Normal**. This means that all the text you have entered, at the moment, is shown in the Normal paragraph style which is one of the styles available in the NORMAL template. Every document produced by Word has to use a template, and NORMAL is the default. A template contains, both the document page settings and a set of formatting instructions which can be applied to text.

Changing Paragraph Styles

To change the style of a paragraph, do the following:

* Place the cursor (insertion pointer) on the paragraph in question, say the title line

* Left click the Style Status button, and select the **Heading 1** style.

The selected paragraph reformats instantly in bold, and in Arial typeface of point size 16.

With the cursor in the second line of text, select **Heading 3** which reformats the line in Arial 13. Your memo should now look presentable, as shown below.

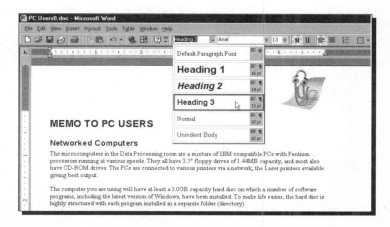

Document Screen Displays

Word provides four display views, Normal, Web Layout, Print Layout, and Outline, as well as the options to view your documents in a whole range of screen enlargements by selecting **Zoom**. You control all these viewing options with the **View** sub-menu, shown here, and when a document is displayed you can switch freely between them. When first loaded the screen displays in Print Layout view.

The view options have the following effect, and can also be accessed by clicking the Views buttons on the left of the Status bar.

Normal Layout

A view that simplifies the layout of the page so that you can type, edit and format text quickly. In normal view, page boundaries, headers and footers, backgrounds, drawing objects, and pictures that do not have the '**In line with text**' wrapping style do not appear.

Web Layout

A view that optimises the layout of a document to make online reading easier. Use this layout view when you are creating a Web page or a document that is viewed on the screen. In Web layout view, you can see backgrounds, text is wrapped to fit the window, and graphics are positioned just as they are in a Web browser.

Print Layout

Provides a WYSIWYG (what you see is what you get) view of a document. The text displays in the typefaces and point sizes you specify, and with the selected attributes.

This view is useful for editing headers and footers, for adjusting margins, and for working with columns and drawing objects. All text boxes or frames, tables, graphics, headers, footers, and footnotes appear on the screen as they will in the final printout.

Outline Layout

Provides a collapsible view of a document, which enables you to see its organisation at a glance. You can display all the text in a file, or just the text that uses the paragraph styles you specify. Using this mode, allows you to quickly rearrange large sections of text. Some people like to create an outline of their document first, consisting of all the headings, then to sort out the document structure and finally fill in the text.

With large documents, you can create what is known as a *Master* document by starting with an Outline View, and then designate headings in the outline as sub-documents. When you save the master document, Word assigns names to each sub-document based on the text you use in the outline headings. You can also convert an existing document to a master document and then divide it into sub-documents, or you can add existing documents to a master document to make them sub-documents.

In a master document, you can quickly change the top-level structure of the document by adding, removing, combining, splitting, renaming, and rearranging sub-documents. You can also create a table of contents, index, cross-references, and headers and footers for all of the sub-documents. The master document's template applies to all the sub-documents, so the entire document has a consistent design. Printing a master document is a fast way to print all the sub-documents without opening them individually. A Master document can be thought of as a 'container' for a set of separate files or sub-documents.

Full Screen

Selecting the **View, Full Screen** command, displays a clean, uncluttered screen; the Toolbars, Ruler, Scroll bars, and Status bar are removed. To return to the usual screen, click the **Close Full Screen** button on the icon which appears at the bottom of your screen when in this mode.

Zoom

Selecting the **View, Zoom** command, displays the Zoom dialogue box (we only show the left side of it here), in which you can change the viewing magnification factor from its default value of 100%.

Changing Default Options

Modifying Margins

To change the standard page margins for your entire document from the cursor position onward, or for selected text (more about this later), do the following:

- Select the **File, Page Setup** command

- Click the left mouse button at the **Margins** tab on the displayed dialogue box, shown below.

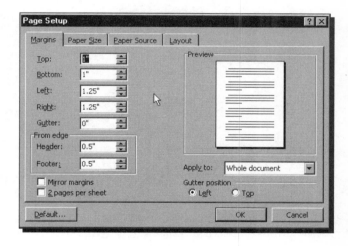

The 'Preview' page to the right of the box shows how your changes will look on a real page.

Changing the Default Paper Size

To change the default paper size from the size set during installation to a different size, do the following:

- Select the **File, Page Setup** command

- Click the left mouse button at the **Paper Size** tab on the displayed dialogue box

- Click the down-arrow against the **Paper Size** box to reveal the list of available paper sizes

- Change the page size to your new choice, and press the **Default** button and confirm that you wish this change to affect all new documents based on the Normal template.

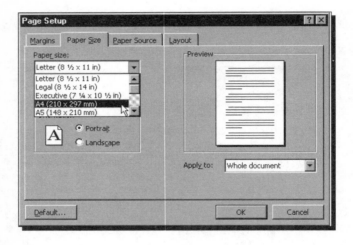

Check that the paper size matches that in your printer, otherwise you may get strange results. The orientation of the printed page is normally **Portrait** (text prints across the page width), but you could choose to change this to **Landscape** which prints across the page length, as long as your printer can print in landscape.

All changes you can make to your document from the Page Setup dialogue box can be applied to either the whole document or to the rest of the document starting from the current position of the insertion pointer. To carry out such changes click the down-arrow button against the **Apply to** box and choose appropriately from the drop-down menu list.

Modifying the Paper Source

Clicking on the third Page Setup tab, displays yet another

dialogue box, part of which is shown here, from which you can select the paper source. You might have a printer that holds paper in trays, in which case you might want to specify that the first page (headed paper perhaps), should be taken from one tray, while the rest of the paper should be taken from a different tray.

Modifying the Page Layout

Clicking the last Page Setup tab displays the Layout box, part

of which is shown here. From this dialogue box you can set options for headers and footers, section breaks, vertical alignment and whether to add line numbers or borders.

The default for **Section Start** is 'New Page' which allows the section to start at the top of the next page. Pressing the down arrow against this option, allows you to change this choice.

In the Headers and Footers section of the dialogue box, you can specify whether you want one header or footer for even-numbered pages and a different header or footer for odd-numbered pages. You can further specify if you want a different header or footer on the first page from the header or footer used for the rest of the document. Word can align the top line with the 'Top' margin, but this can be changed with the **Vertical Alignment** option.

Changing Other Default Options

You can also change the default options available to you in Word 2000, by selecting the **Tools, Options** command. Using the displayed Options dialogue box below, you can, amongst other things, do the following:

* Specify the default **View** options. For example, you can select whether non-printing formatting characters, such as Tabs, Spaces, and Paragraph marks, are shown or not.

* Adjust the **General** Word settings, such as background re-pagination, display of the recently used file-list, and selection of units of measurement.

* Adjust the **Print** settings, such as allowing background printing, reverse print order, or choose to print comments with documents.

* Change the **Save** options, such as selecting to always create a backup copy of your work.

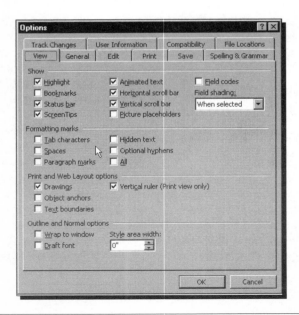

Saving to a File

To save a document to disc, use either of the commands:

- **File, Save** (or click the Save toolbar icon) which is used when a document has previously been saved to disc in a named file; using this command saves your work under the existing filename automatically without prompting you.

- **File, Save As** command which is used when you want to save your document with a different name from the one you gave it already.

Using the **File, Save As** command (or the very first time you use the **File, Save** command when a document has no name), opens the following dialogue box:

Note that the first 255 characters of the first paragraph of a new document is highlighted in the **File name** field box and the program is waiting for you to type a new name. Any name you type (less than 255 characters) will replace the existing name. Filenames cannot include any of the following keyboard characters: /, \, >, <, *, ?, ", |, :, or ;. Word adds the file extension **.doc** automatically and uses it to identify its documents.

You can select a drive other than the one displayed, by clicking the down arrow against the **Save in** text box at the top of the Save As dialogue box. You can also select a folder in which to save your work. If you do not have a suitably named folder, then you can create one using the Create New Folder button on the Save As dialogue box, shown below.

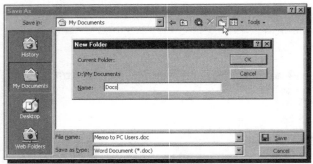

We used this facility to create a folder called **Docs** within the **My Documents** folder.

To save our work currently in memory, we selected the **Docs** folder in the **Save in** field of the Save As dialogue box, then moved the cursor into the **File name** box, and typed **PC Users1**. We suggest you do the same.

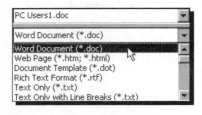

By clicking the **Save as type** button at the bottom of the Save As dialogue box, you can save the Document Template, or the Text Only parts of your work, or you can save your document in a variety of other formats, including Rich Text, and Web Page (HTML).

Selecting File Location

You can select where Word is to look automatically for your document files when you first choose to open or save a document by selecting the **Tools, Options** command, click the File Locations tab of the displayed Options dialogue box, and modify the location of the document files, as shown below.

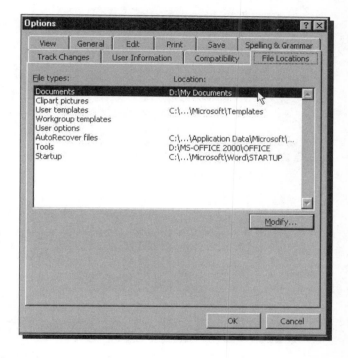

As you can see, the default location of other types of files is also given in the above dialogue box.

Microsoft suggests that you store documents, worksheets, presentations, databases, and other files you are currently working on, in the **My Documents** folder. This, of course, is a matter of preference, so we leave it to you to decide. We prefer to create sub-folders within the **My Documents** folder and save files from the same application in one sub-folder.

Document Properties

A useful feature in Word is the facility to add document properties to every file by selecting the **File, Properties** command. A Properties box, as shown below, opens for you to type additional information about your document.

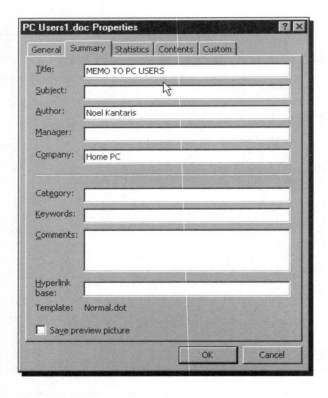

In this box you can select to add a manager, company, or category name to group files together for ease of retrieval.

To do this on a more regular basis, make sure that the **Prompt for Document Properties** box in the Save Options dialogue box (use the **Tools, Options** command and click the Save tab of the Options dialogue box) is selected and appears ticked.

Closing a Document

There are several ways to close a document in Word. Once you have saved it you can click its 'X' close button, or double-click on the Document Control button at the left end of the menu bar; you would usually use these when you have several files open together.

If you want to close the current document, and then open a new one or a different one, do the following:

- Choose **File, Close** to close the current document (remove it from your computer's memory) before using either

- **File, New** (or clicking ▢) to create a new file, or

- **File, Open** (or clicking ▣) to use an existing file.

If the document (or file) has changed since the last time it was saved, you will be given the option to save it before it is removed from memory.

If a document is not closed before a new document is opened, then both documents will be held in memory, but only one will be the current document. To find out which documents are held in memory, look at the Taskbar, or use the **Window** command to reveal the following menu options:

In this case, the third document in the list is the current document, and to make another document the current one, either type the document number, or point at its name and click the left mouse button.

To close a document which is not the current document, use the **Window** command, make it current, and close it with one of the above methods.

Opening a Document

You can use the Open dialogue box in Word, shown below, to open documents that might be located in different locations.

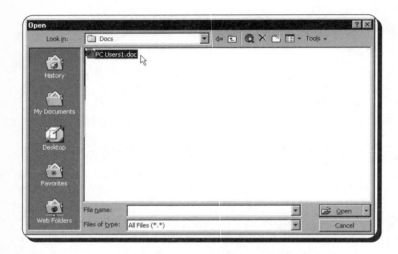

For example, you can open a document which might be on your computer's hard disc, or on a network drive that you have a connection to. To locate other drives, simply click the Up One Level button pointed to below.

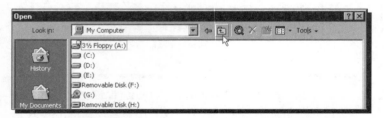

Having selected a drive, you can then select the folder within which your document was saved, select its filename and click the **Open** button on the dialogue box. In our case, the file **PC Users1** is located on the C: drive, in the **My Documents\Docs** folder.

4

Editing Word Documents

It will not be long, when using Word, before you will need to edit your document. One of the first things you will notice is that misspelled words are unobtrusively underlined in a red wavy line and that ungrammatical phrases are similarly underlined in green. To demonstrate this facility, use the **File, New** command (or click ☐) to create a new file, and type the words 'Computors are fun to usr', exactly as misspelled here. What should appear on your screen is shown below, but with the misspelled words underlined in a red wavy line.

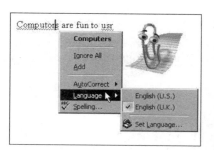

Right-clicking the first word allows you to correct it, as shown here. To correct such a word, left-click on 'Computers'. You even have a choice of English. Next, place the cursor on 'usr' and right-click once more to display:

This is possibly the most timesaving enhancement in editing misspelled words as you type. The spell and grammar checker will be discussed later in more detail.

Other editing could include deleting unwanted words or adding extra text in the document. All these operations are very easy to carry out. For small deletions, such as letters or words, the easiest method is to use the <Del> or <BkSp> keys.

With the <Del> key, position the cursor on the left of the first letter you want to delete and press <Del>. With the <BkSp> key, position the cursor immediately to the right of the character to be deleted and press <BkSp>. In both cases the rest of the line moves to the left to take up the space created by the deleting process.

Word processing is usually carried out in the insert mode. Any characters typed will be inserted at the cursor location (insertion point) and the following text will be pushed to the right, and down, to make room. To insert blank lines in your text, place the cursor at the beginning of the line where the blank line is needed and press <Enter>. To remove the blank line, position the cursor on it and press <Del>.

When larger scale editing is needed you have several alternatives. You could first 'select' the text to be altered, then use the **Cut**, **Copy** and **Paste** operations available in the **Edit** sub-menu, or click on the Toolbar button alternatives shown here.

Another method of copying or moving text is to use the 'drag and drop' facility which requires you to highlight a word, grab it with the left mouse button depressed, and drop it in the required place in your text. This facility will also be discussed shortly in some detail.

Adding Buttons to the Standard Toolbar

When you first use Word, the **Cut** button shown above is not on the default Standard Toolbar. To place it there, first click the **More Buttons** icon, then the **Add or Remove Buttons**,  and from the displayed menu select the one required, as shown to the left. From then on, this button will appear on the Toolbar, but may displace other buttons.

Selecting Text

The procedure in Word, as with most Windows based applications, is first to select the text to be altered before any operation, such as formatting or editing, can be carried out on it. Selected text is highlighted on the screen. This can be carried out in two main ways:

A. Using the keyboard, to select:

- A block of text.

  Position the cursor on the first character to be selected and hold down the <Shift> key while using the arrow keys to highlight the required text, then release the <Shift> key.

- From the present position to the end of the line.

  Use <Shift+End>.

- From the present cursor position to the beginning of the line.

  Use <Shift+Home>.

- From the present cursor position to the end of the document.

  Use <Shift+Ctrl+End>.

- From the present cursor position to the beginning of the document.

  Use <Shift+Ctrl+Home>.

B. With the mouse, to select:

* A block of text.

Press down the left mouse button at the beginning of the block and while holding it pressed, drag the cursor across the block so that the desired text is highlighted, then release the mouse button.

* A word.

Double-click within the word.

* A line.

Place the mouse pointer on the selection bar, just to the left of the line, and click once (for multiple lines, after selecting the first line, drag the pointer in the selection bar).

* A sentence.

Hold the <Ctrl> key down and click in the sentence.

* A paragraph.

Place the mouse pointer in the selection bar and double-click (for multiple paragraphs, after selecting the first paragraph, drag the pointer in the selection bar) or triple-click in the paragraph.

* The whole document.

Place the mouse pointer in the selection bar, hold the <Ctrl> key down and click once.

Copying Blocks of Text

Once text has been selected it can be copied to another location in your present document, to another Word document, or to another Windows application, via the clipboard. As with most of the editing and formatting operations there are several alternative ways of doing this, as follows:

* Use the **Edit, Copy** command sequence from the menu, to copy the selected text to the Windows clipboard, moving the cursor to the start of where you want the copied text to be placed, and using the **Edit, Paste** command.

* Use the quick key combinations, <Ctrl+Ins> (or <Ctrl+C>) to copy and <Shift+Ins> (or <Ctrl+V>) to paste, once the text to be copied has been selected. This does not require the menu bar to be activated.

* Use the 'Copy to clipboard' and 'Paste from clipboard' Standard Toolbar buttons; you can of course only use this method with a mouse.

To copy the same text again to another location, or to any open document window or application, move the cursor to the new location and paste it there with any of these methods. It is stored on the clipboard until it is replaced by the next Cut, or Copy operation.

* Selected text can be copied by holding the <Ctrl> key

depressed while dragging the mouse with the left button held down. The drag pointer is an arrow with an attached square - the vertical dotted line showing the point of insertion. The new text will insert itself where placed, even if the overstrike mode is in operation. Text copied by this method is not placed on the clipboard, so multiple copies are not possible as with other methods.

Moving Blocks of Text

Selected text can be moved to any location in the same document by either of the following:

- Using the **Edit, Cut,** command or <Shift+Del> (or <Ctrl+X>).

- Clicking the 'Cut to clipboard' Standard Toolbar button, shown here.

Next, move the cursor to the required new location and use either of the following procedures:

- The **Edit, Paste** command.

- Any other paste actions as described previously.

The moved text will be placed at the cursor location and will force any existing text to make room for it. This operation can be cancelled by simply pressing <Esc>. Once moved, multiple copies of the same text can be produced by other **Paste** operations.

Selected text can be moved by dragging the mouse with the left button held down. The drag pointer is an arrow with an attached square - the vertical dotted line showing the point of insertion.

Deleting Blocks of Text

When text is 'cut' it is removed from the document, but placed on the clipboard until further text is either copied or cut. With Word any selected text can be deleted by pressing **Edit, Cut,** or clicking the 'Cut to Clipboard' Standard Toolbar icon, shown here, or by pressing the <Del>, or <BkSp> keys. However, using **Edit, Cut**, allows you to use the **Edit, Paste** command, but using the <Del> or <BkSp> keys, does not.

The Undo Command

As text is lost with the delete command, you should use it with caution, but if you do make a mistake all is not lost as long as you act promptly. The **Edit, Undo** command or <Ctrl+Z> (or <Alt+BkSp>) reverses your most recent editing or formatting commands.

You can also use the Undo Standard Toolbar button, shown here, to undo one of several editing or formatting mistakes (press the down arrow to the right of the button to see a list of your recent changes, as shown here).

Undo does not reverse any action once editing changes have been saved to file. Only editing done since the last save can be reversed.

Finding and Changing Text

Word allows you to search for specifically selected text, or character combinations. To do this use the **Find** or the **Replace** option from the **Edit** command sub-menu.

Using the **Find** option (<Ctrl+F>), will highlight each occurrence of the supplied text in turn so that you can carry out some action on it, such as change its font or appearance.

Using the **Replace** option (<Ctrl+H>), allows you to specify what replacement is to be automatically carried out. For example, in a long article you may decide to replace every occurrence of the word 'microcomputers' with the word 'PCs'.

To illustrate the **Replace** procedure, either select the option from the **Edit** sub-menu or use the quick key combination <Ctrl+H>. This opens the Find and Replace dialogue box shown on the next page.

Clicking the **More** button displays the top half of the composite screen dump shown below.

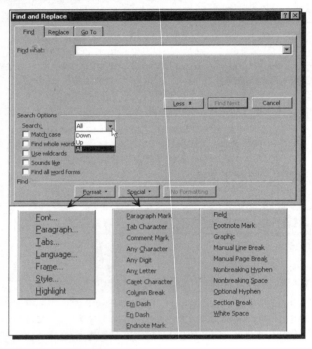

Towards the bottom of the dialogue box, there are five check boxes; the first two can be used to match the case of letters in the search string, and/or a whole word, while the last three can be used for wildcard, 'sounds like' or 'word forms' matching.

The two buttons, **Format** and **Special**, situated at the bottom of the dialogue box, let you control how the search is carried out. The lists of available options, when either of these buttons is pressed, are displayed above. You will of course only see one or the other, but not both as shown here.

You can force both the search and the replace operations to work with exact text attributes. For example, selecting:

- The **Font** option from the list under **Format**, displays a dialogue box in which you select a font (such as Arial, Times New Roman, etc.); a font-style (such as regular, bold, italic, etc.); an underline option (such as single, double, etc.); and special effects (such as strike-through, superscript, subscript, etc.).

- The **Paragraph** option, lets you control indentation, spacing (before and after), and alignment.

- The **Style** option, allows you to search for, or replace, different paragraph styles. This can be useful if you develop a new style and want to change all the text of another style in a document to use your preferred style.

Using the **Special** button, you can search for, and replace, various specified document marks, tabs, hard returns, etc., or a combination of both these and text, as listed in the previous screen dump.

Below we list only two of the many key combinations of special characters that could be typed into the **Find what** and **Replace with** boxes when the **Use wildcards** box is checked.

Type	*To find or replace*
?	Any single character within a pattern. For example, searching for nec?, will find <u>neck</u>, con<u>nect</u>, etc.
*	Any string of characters. For example, searching for c*r, will find such words as <u>cellar</u>, <u>chillier</u>, etc., also parts of words such as <u>chara</u>cter, and combinations of words such as <u>connect, cellar</u>.

Page Breaks

The program automatically inserts a 'soft' page break in a document when a page of typed text is full. To force a manual, or hard page break, either type <Ctrl+Enter> or use the **Insert**, **Break** command and select **Page Break** in the dialogue box, as shown to the left.

Pressing **OK** places a series of dots across the page to indicate the page break (this can only be seen in Normal View, as shown below. If you are in Print View, the second paragraph below appears on the next page. To delete manual page breaks place the cursor on the line of dots, and press the <Del> key. In Print View, place the cursor at the beginning of the second page and press the <BkSp> key.

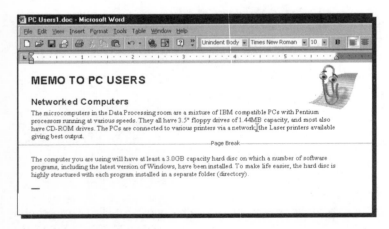

Soft page breaks which are automatically entered by the program at the end of pages, cannot be deleted.

Using the Spell Checker

The package has a very comprehensive spell checker which whenever it thinks it has found a misspelled word, underlines it with a red wavy line. To correct your document, right-click such words for alternatives.

However, the spell checker can also be used in another way. To spell check your document, either click the 'Spelling' button on the Standard Toolbar, shown here, or use the **Tools**, **Spelling and Grammar** command (or **F7**) to open the dialogue box shown below (if necessary, use the **Tools, Language, Set Language** command, select the correct dictionary and click the **Default** button).

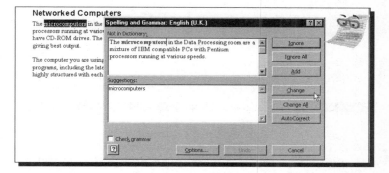

Word starts spell checking from the point of insertion onwards. If you want to spell check the whole document, move the insertion pointer to the beginning of the document before starting. If you want to check a word or paragraph only, highlight it first. Once Word has found a misspelled word, you can either correct it in the Not in Dictionary box, or select a word from the **Suggestions** list.

The main dictionary cannot be edited. However, the system has the ability to add specialised and personal dictionaries with the facility to customise and edit them. If you are using a personal dictionary and choose **Add**, the specified word is added to that dictionary.

Using the Thesaurus

If you are not sure of the meaning of a word, or you want to use an alternative word in your document, then the thesaurus is an indispensable tool. To use the thesaurus, simply place the cursor on the word you want to look up and select **Tools, Language, Thesaurus** command (or press the <Shift+**F7**> key combination). As long as the word is recognised, the following dialogue box will open.

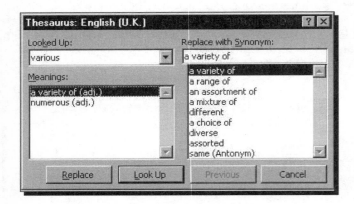

This is very powerful tool. You can see information about an item in the **Meanings** list, or you can look up a synonym in the **Replace with Synonym** list. To change the word in the **Looked Up** text box, select an offered word in either the **Meanings** or the **Replace with Synonym** list box, or type a word directly into the **Replace with Synonym** text box, and press the **Replace** button.

You can use the thesaurus like a simple dictionary by typing any word into the **Replace with Synonym** box and clicking the **Look Up** button. If the word is recognised, lists of its meaning variations and synonyms will be displayed. Pressing the **Replace** button will place the word into the document.

The Grammar Checker

The Grammar Checker provided with Word is much better than that of previous versions of the package, but you must first customise it to your requirements. This will be explained shortly with an example.

To illustrate the use of the Grammar Checker, open the **PC Users1** file and at the end of it type the following sentence which we know will cause reaction from the grammar checker.

'Use the My Computer utility which Microsoft have spent much time and effort making as intuitive as possible.'

Next, select the **Tools**, **Spelling and Grammar** command. Once the spelling has been ckecked, the Grammar Checker underlines the words 'utility which' with a green wavy line as shown below.

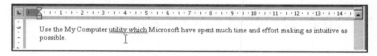

Right-clicking the wavy line opens a shortcut menu and choosing the **Grammar** option displays the following:

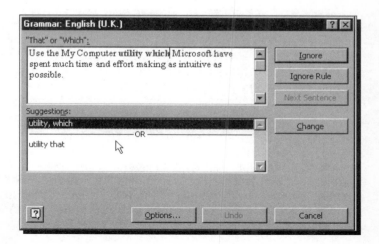

The Grammar Checker has picked up what is incorrect, as expected. No other errors were flagged up in this memo. Gone are the messages about 'Passive Verb Usage' which was the obsession of the Grammar Checker in previous versions of Word.

With this Grammar Checker, you have the choice of five pre-set types of writing styles, namely 'Casual', 'Standard', 'Formal', 'Technical', and 'Custom', as shown below - use the **Tools**, **Options** command to open the dialogue box.

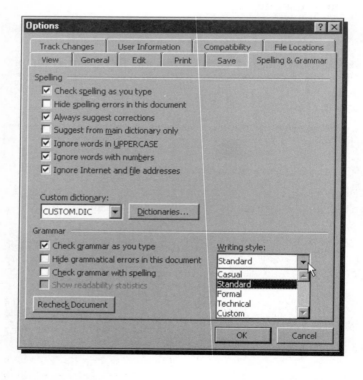

As you can see, you will need to spend quite some time customising the way the grammar checker works. For example, clicking the **Settings** button in the above dialogue box (obscured by the drop-down **Writing style** menu), displays the following Grammar Settings dialogue box.

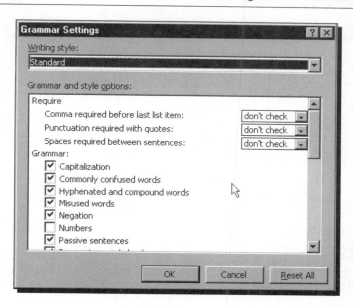

Do spend some time with this dialogue box to find out all the available options before going on.

Printing Documents

When Windows was first installed on your computer the printers you intend to use should have been selected, and

the SETUP program should have installed the appropriate printer drivers. Before printing for the first time, you would be wise to ensure that your printer is in fact properly installed. To do this, click on **Start** then select **Settings** and click the **Printers** menu option to open the Printers dialogue box shown to the left.

Here, two printer drivers have been installed; an HP LaserJet 5MP as the 'default' printer and an HP LaserJet 5/5M PostScript. In our case these are both configured to output to a printer via the parallel port LPT1. This refers to the socket at the back of your PC which is connected to your printer. LPT1 is short for Line Printer No. 1. Your selections may, obviously, not be the same.

To see how a printer is configured (whether to print to the parallel port or to a file), select it by clicking its icon, use the **File, Properties** command and click the Details tab of the displayed dialogue box.

Next, return to or reactivate Word and, if the document you want to print is not in memory, either click the Open button on the Toolbar, or use the **File, Open** command, to display the Open dialogue box, as described at the end of the previous chapter. Use this dialogue box to locate the file (document) you want to print, which will be found on the drive and folder (directory) on which you saved it originally.

To print your document, do one of the following:

- Click the Print icon on the Standard Toolbar, shown here, which prints the document using the current defaults.

- Use the **File, Print** command which opens the 'Print' box, shown below.

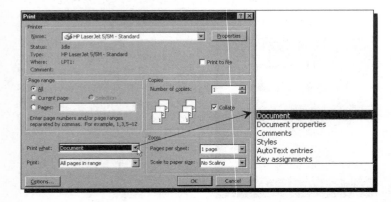

The settings in the Print dialogue box allow you to select the number of copies, and which pages, you want printed. You can also select to print the document, the summary information relating to that document, comments, styles, etc., as shown in the drop-down list also on the previous page.

You can even change the selected printer by clicking the down arrow against the **Printer Name** box which displays the available printers on your system.

Clicking the **Properties** button on the Print dialogue box, displays the Properties dialogue box for the selected printer, shown below, which allows you to select the paper size, orientation needed, paper source, etc.

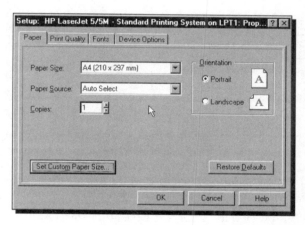

The **Options** button on the Print dialogue box, gives you access to some more advanced print options, such as printing in reverse order, with or without comments, print hidden text or field codes, etc., as shown on the next page.

Clicking the **OK** button on these various multilevel dialogue boxes, causes Word to accept your selections and return you to the previous level dialogue box, until the Print dialogue box is reached. Selecting **OK** on this first level dialogue box, sends print output from Word to your selection, either the printer connected to your computer, or to an encoded file on disc. Selecting **Cancel** or **Close** on any level dialogue box, aborts the selections made at that level.

Do remember that, whenever you change printers, the appearance of your document may change, as Word uses the fonts available with the newly selected printer. This can affect the line lengths, which in turn will affect both the tabulation and pagination of your document.

Before printing to paper, click the Print Preview icon (if not on the Standard Toolbar, click the More Buttons icon or use the **File, Print Preview** command, to see how much of your document will fit on your selected page size. This depends very much on the chosen font. Thus, this option allows you to see the layout of the final printed page, which can save a few trees and equally important to you, a lot of frustration and wear and tear on your printer. To return to your working document from a print preview display, click the **Close** button on its menu bar.

Other enhancements of your document, such as selection of fonts, formatting of text, and pagination, will be discussed in the next chapter.

5

Formatting Word Documents

Formatting involves the appearance of individual words or even characters, the line spacing and alignment of paragraphs, and the overall page layout of the entire document. These functions are carried out in Word in several different ways.

Primary page layout is included in a document's Template and text formatting in a Template's styles. Within any document, however, you can override Paragraph Style formats by applying text formatting and enhancements manually to selected text. To immediately cancel manual formatting, select the text and use the **Edit, Undo** command, or (<Ctrl+Z>). The selected text reverts to its original format. In the long term, you can cancel manual formatting by selecting the text and using the <Shift+Ctrl+N> key stroke. The text then reverts to its style format.

Formatting Text

If you use TrueType fonts, which are automatically installed when you set up Windows, Word uses the same font to display text on the screen and to print on paper. The screen fonts provide a very close approximation of printed characters. TrueType font names are preceded by ℡ in the Font box on the Formatting Bar and in the Font dialogue box which displays when you use the **Format, Font** command.

If you use non-TrueType fonts, then use a screen font that matches your printer font. If a matching font is not available, or if your printer driver does not provide screen font information, Windows chooses the screen font that most closely resembles the printer font.

Originally, the title and subtitle of the **PC Users1** memo, were selected from the default Normal style as 'Heading 1' and 'Heading 3', which were in the 16 and 13 point size Arial typeface, respectively, while the main text was typed in 10 point size Times New Roman.

To change this memo into what appears on the screen dump displayed below, first select the title of the memo and format it to italics, 18 point size Arial and centre it between the margins, then select the subtitle and format it to 14 point size Arial. Both title and subtitle are in bold as part of the definition of their respective paragraph style. Finally select each paragraph of the main body of the memo in turn, and format it to 12 point size Times New Roman. If you can't access these font styles, it will probably be because your printer does not support them, in which case you will need to select other fonts that are supported.

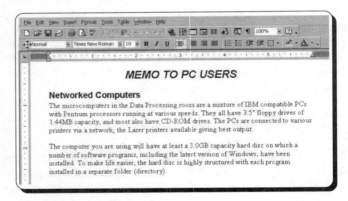

All of this formatting can be achieved by using the buttons on the Formatting Bar (see also the section entitled 'Paragraph Alignment').

As you can see, by moving the Formatting Bar from its former position (to the right of the Standard Toolbar) to just below it (see next section on how to do this), we have exposed more buttons.

Save the result under the new filename **PC Users2**, using the **File, Save As** command.

Moving Toolbars

As we have seen, the default buttons appearing on the two Toolbars below the Menu Bar have distinctive functions. The one to the left is the Standard Toolbar, while the one to the right is the Formatting Bar. Each of these two Toolbars is preceded by a vertical handle. Moving the mouse pointer on such a handle, changes it into a small four-headed 'moving' pointer, as shown below.

It is in fact possible to move individual Toolbar sets to any part of the screen, and also change the buttons contained in each. As an example, we will move the Formatting Bar and place it below the Standard Toolbar. To do so, move the mouse pointer on to the vertical handle preceding the set you want to move, and when it changes into the small four-headed pointer press the left mouse button and drag it below its current position. Releasing the mouse button, fixes the bar into its new position, as shown below.

As you can see, additional buttons have appeared on both bars, which previously could not be seen.

To see additional sets of Toolbars, use the **View, Toolbars** command to open up a menu of options, as shown to the left. You can toggle these on and off by clicking on their names. Be careful, however, how many of these you activate, as they take valuable screen space.

Text Enhancements

In Word all manual formatting, including the selection of font, point size, style (bold, italic, highlight, strike-through, hidden and capitals), colour, super/subscript, and various underlines, are carried out by first selecting the text and then executing the formatting command.

The easiest way of activating the formatting commands is from the Formatting Bar. Another way is to use the **Format**, **Font** command, which displays the following dialogue box:

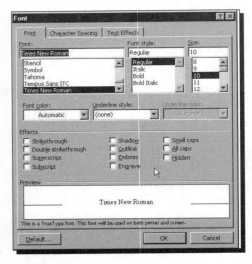

Yet another method is by using quick keys, some of which are listed below:

To Format	*Type*
Bold	Ctrl+B
Italic	Ctrl+I
Underline	Ctrl+U
Word underline	Ctrl+Shift+W
Double underline	Ctrl+Shift+D

There are quick keys to do almost anything, but the problem is remembering them! The ones listed here are the most useful and the easiest to remember.

Paragraph Alignment

Word defines a paragraph, as any text which is followed by a paragraph mark, which is created by pressing the <Enter> key. So single line titles, as well as long typed text, can form paragraphs.

 The paragraph symbol, shown here, is only visible in your text if you have selected it from the Standard Toolbar, or used <Ctrl+*>.

Word allows you to align a paragraph at the left margin (the default), at the right margin, centred between both margins, or justified between both margins. As with most operations there are several ways to perform alignment in Word. Three such methods are:

- Using buttons on the **Formatting Bar**.

- Using keyboard short cuts, when available.

- Using the **Format**, **Paragraph** menu command.

The table below describes the buttons on the Formatting Bar and their keystroke shortcuts.

Buttons on Formatting Bar	*Paragraph Alignment*	*Keystrokes*
	Left	<Ctrl+L>
	Centred	<Ctrl+E>
	Right	<Ctrl+R>
	Justified	<Ctrl+J>

The display below shows the dialogue box resulting from using the **Format**, **Paragraph** command in which you can specify any **Left, Right**, or **Special** indentation required.

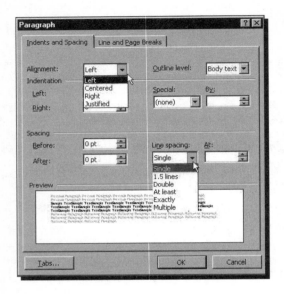

Paragraph Spacing

The above Paragraph dialogue box can also be used to display a paragraph on screen, or print it on paper, in single-line, 1½-line, or double-line spacing. You can even set the spacing to any value you want by using the **At Least** option, as shown on the above screen dump, then specify what interval you want.

The available shortcut keys for paragraph spacing are as follows:

To Format	Type
Single-spaced lines	Ctrl+1
One-and-a-half-spaced lines	Ctrl+5
Double-spaced lines	Ctrl+2

Whichever of the above methods is used, formatting can take place either before or after the text is entered. If formatting is selected first, then text will type in the chosen format until a further formatting command is given. If, on the other hand, you choose to enter text and then format it afterwards, you must first select the text to be formatted, then activate the formatting.

Word gives you the choice of 4 units to work with, inches, centimetres, points or picas. These can be selected by using the **Tools**, **Options** command, choosing the **General** tab of the displayed Options dialogue box, and clicking the down arrow against the **Measurement units** list box, shown open here, which is to be found at the bottom of the dialogue box. We selected to work in centimetres from now on.

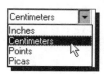

Indenting Text

Most documents will require some form of paragraph indenting. An indent is the space between the margin and the edge of the text in the paragraph. When an indent is set (on the left or right side of the page), any justification on that side of the page sets at the indent, not the page border.

To illustrate indentation, open the file **PC Users2**, select the first paragraph, and then choose the **Format**, **Paragraph** command. In the **Indentation** field, select 2.5cm for both **Left** and **Right**, as shown on the next page. On clicking **OK**, the first selected paragraph is displayed indented. Our screen dump shows the result of the indentation as well as the settings on the Paragraph dialogue box which caused it.

You can also use the Formatting Bar buttons, shown below, to decrease or increase the indent of a selected text.

 Use this button to decrease indent.

 Use this button to increase indent.

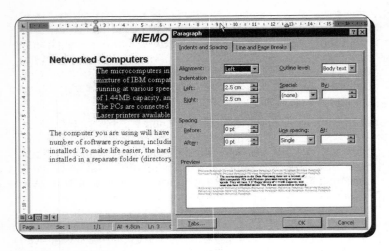

The **Indentation** option in the Paragraph dialogue box, can be used to create 'hanging' indents, where all the lines in a paragraph, including any text on the first line that follows a tab, are indented by a specified amount. This is often used in lists to emphasise certain points.

To illustrate the method, use the **PC Users1** file and add at the end of it the text shown below. After you have typed the text in, save the enlarged memo as **PC Users3**, before going on with formatting the new information.

In Windows you can work with files in three different ways:

Name Description

My Computer Use the My Computer utility which Microsoft have spent much time and effort making as intuitive as possible.

Explorer Use the Windows Explorer, a much-improved version of the older File Manager.

MS-DOS Use an MS-DOS Prompt window if you prefer to and are an expert with the DOS commands.

Saving the work at this stage is done as a precaution in case anything goes wrong with the formatting - it is sometimes much easier to reload a saved file (using the **File, Open** command), than it is to try to unscramble a wrongly formatted document!

Next, highlight the last 4 paragraphs above, use the **Format**, **Paragraph** command, and select 'Hanging' under **Special** and 3 cm under **By**. On clicking the **OK** button, the text formats as shown in the composite screen dump below, but it is still highlighted. To remove the highlighting, click the mouse button anywhere on the page. The second and following lines of the selected paragraphs, should be indented 3 cm from the left margin.

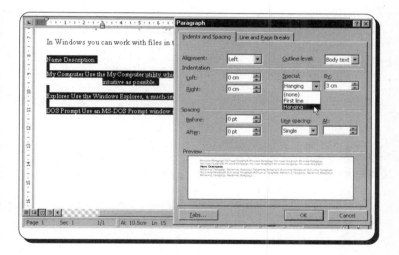

This is still not very inspiring, so to complete the effect we will edit the first lines of each paragraph as follows:

Place the cursor in front of the word 'Description' and press the <Tab> key once. This places the start of the word in the same column as the indented text of the other paragraphs. To complete the effect place tabs before the words 'Use' in the next three paragraphs, until your hanging indents are correct, as shown on the next page.

In Windows you can work with files in three different ways:

Name   Description

My Computer   Use the My Computer utility which Microsoft
                        have spent much time and effort making as
                        intuitive as possible.

Explorer   Use the Windows Explorer, a much-improved
                        version of the older File Manager.

MS-DOS   Use an MS-DOS Prompt window if you prefer
                        to and are an expert with the DOS commands.

This may seem like a complicated rigmarole to go through each time you want the hanging indent effect, but with Word you will eventually set up all your indents, etc., as styles in templates. Then all you do is click in a paragraph to produce them.

 When you finish formatting the document, save it under its current filename either with the **File, Save** command (<Ctrl+S>), or by clicking the Save button. This command does not display a dialogue box, so you use it when you do not need to make any changes to the saving operation.

Inserting Bullets

Bullets are small characters you can insert, anywhere you like, in the text of your document to improve visual impact. In Word there are several choices for displaying lists with bullets or numbers. As well as the two Formatting Bar buttons, others are made available through the **Format, Bullets and Numbering** command, which displays the following dialogue box.

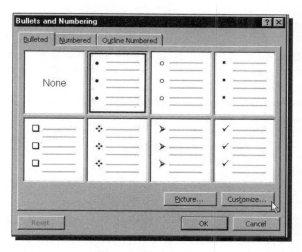

You can select any of the bullets shown here, and then you could click the **Customize** button to change the shape and size of the bullet, or the indentation.

Further, by pressing the **Bullet** button on the Customized Bulleted List dialogue box which would be displayed, you could select any character from the Symbol typeface or other available typefaces.

If you select the **Numbered** or **Outline Numbered** tab, a similar dialogue box is displayed, giving you a choice of several numbering or outline (multilevel) systems.

Once inserted, you can copy, move or cut a bulleted line in the same way as any other text. However, you can not delete a bullet with the <BkSp> or <Del> keys.

Inserting Date and Time

You can insert today's date, the date the current document was created or was last revised, or a date or time that reflects the current system date and time into a document. Therefore, the date can be a date that changes, or a date that always stays the same. In either case, the date is inserted in a date field.

To insert a date field in your document, place the cursor where you want to insert the date, select the **Insert**, **Date and Time** command and choose one of the displayed date formats which suits you from the dialogue box shown below.

Highlighting '27 September, 1999' (or whatever date is current), and pressing **OK**, inserts the date in our document at the chosen position.

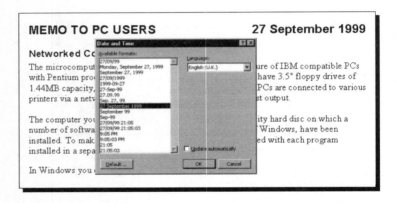

The above screen is a composite of the operation required and the result of that operation.

If you save a document with a date field in it and you open it a few days later, the date shown on it will be the original date the document was created. Should you want to update this date to the current date, select the **Insert**, **Date and Time** command and check the **Update automatically** box, then click the **OK** button.

Inserting Annotations

Another powerful feature of Word is the facility to add comments to a document. These act like electronic labels, initialled by the people who might have an input to a document, as shown below.

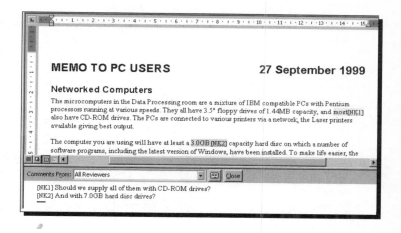

To add comments to a document, place the cursor at the place you want to add a comment (or highlight a portion of text), and use the **Insert**, **Comment** command.

Each person who views and edits the same document is normally identified by **A1**, **A2**, etc., which are used to mark the place in the text where a comment is required. A separate comment pane holds the actual comments. In our case instead of **A1**, etc., different initials are being used which were declared by using the **Tools**, **Options** command and clicking on the **User Information** tab on the Options dialogue box which displays what is shown on the next page.

It is in this dialogue box that you register your user name, initials to be used in the main text while your comments are typed in the 'comments' pane against your numbered initials, and your mailing address.

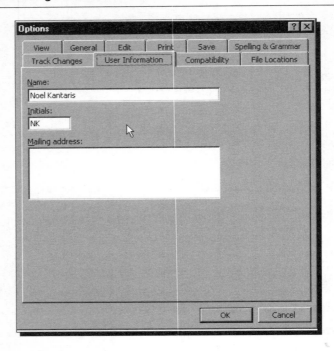

You can read inserted comments, by simply pointing to the marked word within the document. A second later a yellow banner is displayed with the actual comment in it. To change or delete a comment, right-click the marked text, then select what you want to do from the quick menu, as shown below.

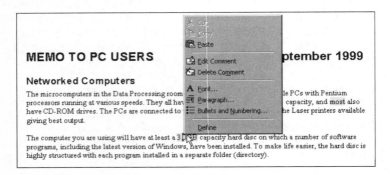

Formatting with Page Tabs

You can format text in columns by using tab stops. Word has default left tab stops every 1.27 cm from the left margin, as shown here. This symbol appears on the left edge of the ruler (see below).

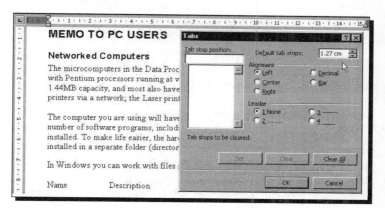

To set tabs, use either the **Format**, **Tabs** command which produces the Tabs dialogue box, or click on the tab symbol on the left of the Ruler which cycles through the available tab stops.

The tab stop types available have the following functions:

Button	Name	Effect
	Left	Left aligns text after the tab stop.
	Centre	Centres text on tab stop.
	Right	Right aligns text after the tab stop.
	Decimal	Aligns decimal point with tab stop.

To clear the ruler of tab settings press the **Clear All** button in the Tabs dialogue box. When you set a tab stop on the ruler, all default tab stops to the left of the one you are setting are removed. In addition, tab stops apply either to the paragraph containing the cursor, or to any selected paragraphs.

The easiest way to set a tab is to click on the tab type button you want and then point and click at the required position on the lower half of the ruler. To remove an added tab, point to it, click and drag it off the ruler.

If you want tabular text to be separated by characters instead of by spaces, select one of the three available characters from the **Leader** box in the Tabs dialogue box. The options are none (the default), dotted, dashed, or underline. The Contents pages of this book are set with right tabs and dotted leader characters.

Note: As all paragraph formatting, such as tab stops, is placed at the end of a paragraph, if you want to carry the formatting of the current paragraph to the next, press <Enter>. If you don't want formatting to carry on, press the down arrow key instead.

Formatting with Styles

We saw earlier on page 43, how you can format your work using Paragraph Styles, but we confined ourselves to using the default **Normal** styles only. In this section we will get to grips with how to create, modify, use, and manage styles.

As mentioned previously, a Paragraph Style is a set of formatting instructions which you save so that you can use it repeatedly within a document or in different documents. A collection of Paragraph Styles can be placed in a Template which could be appropriate for, say, all your memos, so it can be used to preserve uniformity. It maintains consistency and saves time by not having to format each paragraph individually.

Further, should you decide to change a style, all the paragraphs associated with that style reformat automatically. Finally, if you want to provide a pattern for shaping a final document, then you use what is known as a Template. All documents which have not been assigned a document template, use the **Normal.dot** global template, by default.

Paragraph Styles

Paragraph Styles contain paragraph and character formats and a name can be attached to these formatting instructions. From then on, applying the style name is the same as formatting that paragraph with the same instructions.

You can create a style by example, using either the Formatting Bar or the keyboard, or you can create a style from scratch, before you use it, by selecting the **Format, Style** menu command. By far the simplest way of creating a style is by example.

Creating Paragraph Styles by Example: Previously, we spent some time manually creating some hanging indents in the last few paragraphs of the **PC Users3** document. To create a style from this previous work, place the insertion pointer in one of these paragraphs, say, in the 'Name Description' line, and highlight the entire name of the existing style in the Formatting Bar's Style box, as shown below.

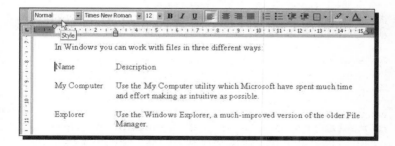

Then, type the new style name you want to create, say, 'Hanging Indent', and press <Enter>.

Finally, highlight the last three paragraphs with hanging indents and change their style to the new 'Hanging Indent', by clicking the mouse in the Style box button and selecting the appropriate style from the displayed list, as shown below. Save the result as **PC Users4**.

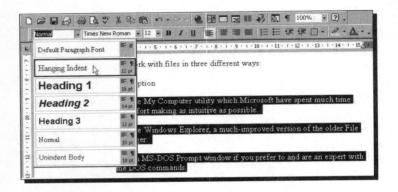

Creating Styles with the Menu Command: You can create, or change, a style before you apply any formatting to a paragraph, by using the **Format**, **Style** command. This displays the Style dialogue box, in which you can choose which style you want to change from the displayed **Styles** list.

Having selected the style you want to change (or not, as the case may be), click the **Modify** button which produces the Modify Style dialogue box. From here you can create a new style, or modify an existing style, by changing the formatting of characters, borders, paragraphs, and tab stops. You can even select which style should follow your current style.

Finally, have a look at Word's built-in styles by selecting **Style Gallery** from the **Format, Theme** menu. There are over sixty available styles, one of which might suite your type of document. Try them with the **PC Users4** file open, as it reformats your document on a viewing pane.

Document Templates

A document template provides the overall pattern of your final document. It can contain:

- Styles to control your paragraph and formats.

- Page set-up options.

- Boilerplate text, which is text that remains the same in every document.

- AutoText, which is standard text and graphics that you could insert in a document by typing the name of the AutoText entry.

- Macros, which are programs that can change the menus and key assignments to comply with the type of document you are creating.

- Customised shortcuts, toolbars and menus.

If you don't assign a template to a document, then the default **Normal.dot** template is used by Word. To create a new document template, you either modify an existing one, create one from scratch, or create one based on the formatting of an existing document.

Creating a Document Template

To illustrate the last point above, we will create a simple document template, which we will call **PC User**, based on the formatting of the **PC Users4** document. But first, make sure you have defined the 'Hanging Indent' style as explained earlier.

To create a template based on an existing document do the following:

- Open the existing document.

- Select the **File, Save As** command which displays the Save As dialogue box, shown overleaf.

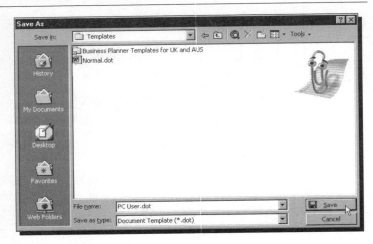

- In the **Save as type** box, select Document Template.

- In the **Save in** box, use the Templates folder which should have opened for you.

- In the **File name** box, type the name of the new template (PC User in our example).

- Press the **Save** button, which opens the template file **PC User.dot** in the Word working area.

- Add the text and graphics you want to appear in all new documents that you base on this template, and *delete* any items (including text) you do not want to appear. In our example, we deleted everything in the document, bar the heading, and added the words 'PC User Group' using **Insert, Picture, WordArt**, to obtain:

- Click the Save icon on the Toolbar, and close the document.

To use the new template, do the following:

- Use the **File**, **New** command which causes the New dialogue box to be displayed, as shown below.

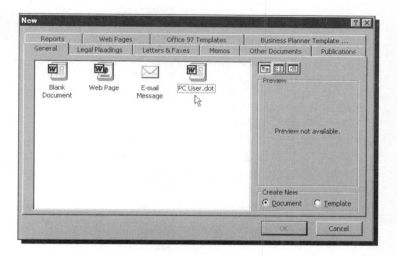

- Click the General tab and select the name of the template you want to use from the displayed list.

- Make sure that the radio button **Document** is selected, and click the **OK** button.

The new document will be using the selected template.

Templates can also contain Macros as well as AutoText; macros allow you to automate Word keystroke actions only, while AutoText speeds up the addition of boilerplate text and graphics into your document. However, the design of these features is beyond the scope of this book.

On the other hand, Word has a series of built-in templates to suit every occasion. These can be found, as seen in the above dialogue box, under the tabs of Letters & Faxes, Memos, Reports, etc. If you upgraded from Office 97, you even have its templates for your use. Try looking at some of these templates.

Special Formatting Features

Word has several special formatting features which force text to override style and style sheet formatting. In what follows, we discuss the most important amongst these.

Changing the Default Character Format

As we have seen, for all new documents Word uses the Times New Roman type font with a 12 points size as the default for the Normal style, which is contained in the Normal template. If the majority of your work demands some different font style or size, then you can change these defaults to suit yourself.

To change the default character formatting, use the **Format**, **Font** command, select the new defaults you want to use, and press the **Default** button, as shown below:

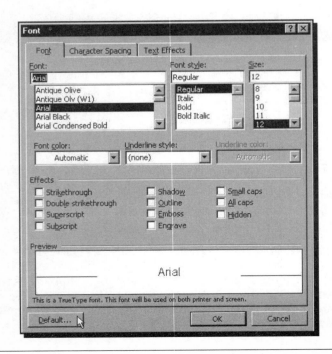

On pressing the **Default** button, The Help Assistant displays the following warning:

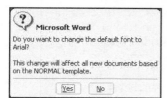

Pressing the **Yes** button, changes the default character settings for this and all subsequent new documents, but does not change already existing ones.

Inserting Special Characters and Symbols

Word has a collection of Symbol fonts, such as the characters produced by the Symbol, Webdings, and Wingdings character sets, from which you can select characters and insert them into your document using the **Insert, Symbol** command. When this command is executed, Word displays the following dialogue box:

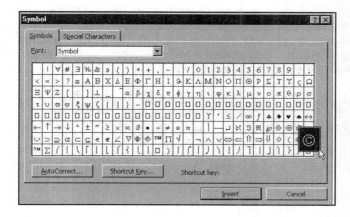

Pressing the down-arrow button next to the **Font** box, reveals the other available character sets. The set showing above is the Symbol set. If you point and click the left mouse button at a character within the set, it selects it and magnifies the selected character. If you double-click the left mouse button, it transfers the selected character to your document at the insertion point.

A Symbol character can be deleted with the <Del> key if you press it twice, or if you press the <BkSp> key once. The advantage of using Symbol is that Word embeds codes in your document which prevent you from changing the character by selecting it and changing to a different font. Thus, this type of formatting overrides any changes you might introduce with a new paragraph formatting.

Inserting Other Special Characters

You can include other special characters in a document, such as optional hyphens, which remain invisible until they are needed to hyphenate a word at the end of a line; non-breaking hyphens, which prevent unwanted hyphenation; non-breaking spaces, which prevent two words from splitting at the end of a line; or opening and closing single quotes.

There are two ways you could use to insert such special characters in your document. One is to click at the **Special Characters** tab of the Symbol dialogue box which reveals a long list of these special characters, as shown below, select one of them and click the **Insert** button. The other way is to use the default key combination (listed against the special characters of the Symbol dialogue box), which does not require you to open it in the first place.

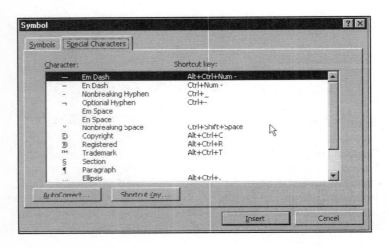

6

Document Enhancements

In this section we discuss features that enhance a document's appearance, such as page numbering, use of headers and footers, use of footnotes, how to create a document with multiple columns, how to incorporate text boxes, and how to import pictures into frames.

Page Numbering

If you need to number the pages of a document, but not the first page, use the **Insert, Page Numbers** command, which displays the following dialogue box:

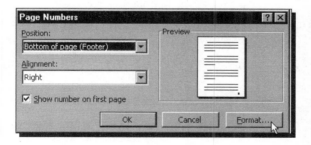

Use this box to specify the position of the page numbers in your document and their alignment. You can also select whether to **Show number on first page** or not. Clicking the **Format** button, opens the adjacent Page Number Format dialogue box.

From this last dialogue box you can select the **Number format** from the following alternatives, '1, a, A, i, or I'; the more usual style being the first option, as used in this book. The 'Page numbering' option gives you two alternatives; **Continue from previous section**, or **Start at** a specified number.

To illustrate page numbering, open the **PC Users4** document and use the **Insert, Page Numbers** command. Then, select 'Center' from the **Alignment** list box and make sure that the **Show number on First page** box is ticked. Next, press the **Format** button, select **Start at 1** at the bottom of the second dialogue box, and click the **OK** button on each dialogue box. The result is a number '1' appearing centrally in a footer at the bottom of page 1, as shown below.

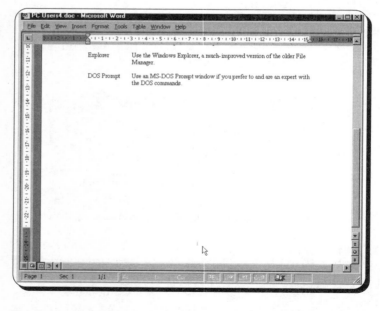

To display the above as shown, we used the **View, Toolbars** command and unchecked in turn the options **Standard**, and **Formatting**. We also used the **View, Zoom**, 75% command. Finally, save the current document as **PC Users5**.

Using Headers and Footers

Headers consist of text placed in the top margin area of a page, whereas footers are text in the bottom margin. Simple headers or footers in Word can consist of text and a page number, which are produced in the same position of every page in a document, while more complicated ones can also contain graphics images.

Word allows you to have one header/footer for the first page of a document, or section of a document, and a different one for the rest of the document. It also allows you to select a different header or footer for odd or even pages.

To insert a header or footer in a document, select the **View, Header and Footer** command, which causes Word to display the following:

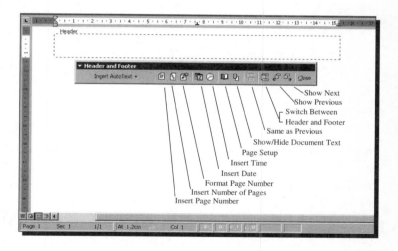

From here you can either click the **Insert AutoText** button to access one of the displayed options to automatically insert information on headers and footers, or you can use the individual buttons which gives you more control of the inserted information.

For example, you can insert a page number and format it, insert the current date and time, or use the page set-up option to create a different header or footer for the first page of a document, or create different headers and footers for odd and even pages. You can also show and hide the document text, create similar headers and footers in a section to those of a previous section, or jump to the previous or next header and footer.

In the example below, we chose to click the 'Insert Date' button on the Header and Footer Bar, then we pressed <Tab> and typed 'Chapter 6' in the middle of the header panel, then we pressed <Tab> and clicked the 'Insert Time' button.

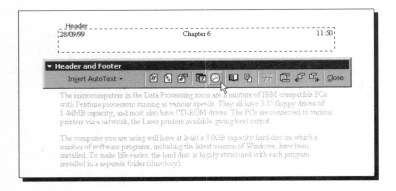

Once you select the **Close** button, headers and footers can be formatted and edited like any other text. To edit a header or footer, simply point to the appropriate panel and double-click. The Header and Footer Bar will appear on the screen and from then on you can use the editing and formatting commands, or the buttons available to you on the Formatting Toolbar. Note that the styles for headers and footers are named by Word automatically as 'Header' and 'Footer'. In the above example we increased the font size of the header from 10 to 11.

Using Footnotes

If your document requires footnotes at the end of each page, or end-notes at the end of each chapter, they are very easy to add and later, if necessary, to edit. Place the cursor at the position you want the reference point to be in the document and select **Insert, Footnote**, which opens the following simulated dialogue boxes.

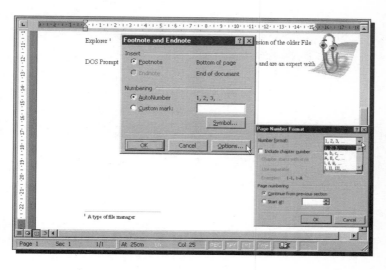

This displays both the two dialogue boxes and the results obtained, on the same screen. The first reference point was placed after the word 'Explorer'. The text for the footnote is typed after pressing the **OK** button of each dialogue box in succession.

The default option in the first dialogue box is **Footnote** and **AutoNumber**. If you choose to press the **Options** button in this box, Word displays the second dialogue box from which you choose the **Number Format**, and the reference to **Start At** a specific number or character, or continue from the previous section. You can also select to include the Chapter number within the referencing style.

If you wanted to type a reference mark of your own choosing, then select the **Custom mark** from the first dialogue box. Pressing the **Symbol** button allows you the use of endless characters, particularly if you choose the 'Symbol' or 'Wingdings' styles in the **Font** list, as shown below.

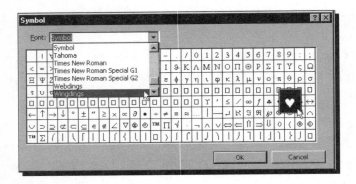

Once you have decided on your selection, save the resultant work under the current filename, **PC Users5**.

Using Multiple Columns on a Page

You can quickly modify the number of displayed columns, either for the whole document or for selected text by using the Columns button from the Toolbar, shown here. However, if you want more control over how the columns are displayed, then use the **Format, Columns** command. Below, we have selected the second paragraph of the **PC Users5** memo and then used the **Format, Columns** command to format it in two columns with 1.27cm in between the two columns.

To see how the 'Preview' page changes, click the appropriate button on the **Presets** field of the Columns dialogue box. Now change the **Spacing** (otherwise known as gutter width) to see how to set the separation zones between columns.

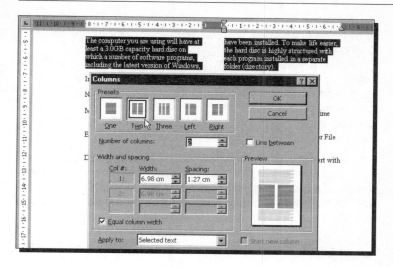

If you want to be able to see the result of your selection on your actual text, use the **View** command and select the **Print Layout** mode. As usual, you will only see your selected text in two columns, after you press the **OK** button on the Columns dialogue box.

Text Boxes and Frames

Word uses both text boxes and frames. These can best be thought of as containers for text that can be positioned on a page and sized.

In earlier versions of Word, only frames were available and were used whenever you wanted to wrap text around a graphic or framed text. In Word 2000, you can wrap text around a graphic of any size or shape without first inserting it in a text box or frame. However, when opening a document created in earlier versions of Word which contains a graphic in a frame, Word opens it with a frame around it.

Text boxes, which were first used in Word 97, provide nearly all the advantages of frames, plus a lot more besides. For example, you can make text flow from one part of a document to another part by linking the text boxes. For most cases, a text box is preferable, but you must use a frame when you want to position text or graphics that contain comments, footnotes or end-notes, fields used for numbering lists and paragraphs in legal documents and outlines, tables of contents and index entries.

It is perhaps worth while at this point spending some time with the Assistant exploring the differences between frames and text boxes. To do so, click on the Assistant and search for information on 'frames'. The Assistant will then display the help screen shown below.

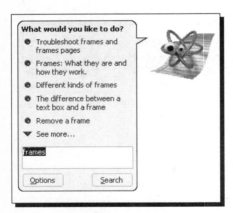

Selecting each item in turn, produces further useful help screens on the subject.

In case you wonder how we got the Assistant to adopt the displayed shape, right-click it and select **Animate!** from the shortcut menu.

Inserting Text Boxes

With Word you can create an empty text box by using the **Insert, Text Box** command. If you are not in Page Layout mode, the program will automatically switch you to it on selection of this command. The program then opens a cross-hair on your display and by moving this to the desired position, then pressing the left mouse button and dragging the mouse, you can insert a text box of the required size in your document, as shown on the next page.

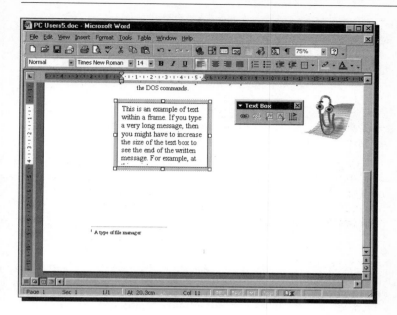

Releasing the left-mouse button, fixes the text box in position in your document with the insertion point blinking in the upper left corner within the text box. When you type text, it wraps to fit the text box, but if you type more lines than can be accommodated within the text box, as in the above example, you will have to increase its vertical size manually to see all the typed text.

Moving Text Boxes

A text box can be moved around your document by first selecting it, then dragging it with the mouse (move the mouse pointer over the edge of the text box until it turns to a four-headed arrow, as shown on the next page, then click and drag to the desired position). The dotted outline shows the position in which the frame will be placed once you let go the left mouse button.

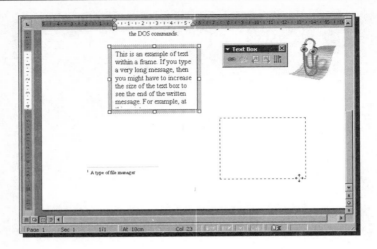

Another way of moving a text box is by first selecting it, then using the **Format, Text Box** command to display the Format Text Box which is shown below with its Layout tab depressed.

Next, click the **Advanced** button to display an additional dialogue box, shown below.

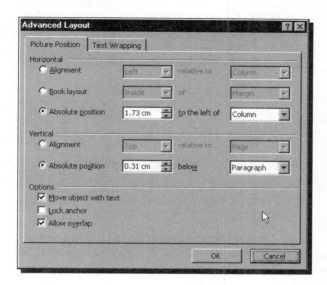

In this dialogue box you can specify the exact position of the text box on the page. You also have the option of anchoring the text box in that exact position, or allowing it to move with the text of the main document.

Pressing the Text Wrapping tab of the Advanced Layout dialogue box, allows you to specify the wrapping options when a text box is placed in the middle of an existing paragraph. If you select a wrapping style other than **Top & bottom**, then format the text into two columns, as discussed on page 105, before inserting the text box - it will look much better. Wrapping style options can be selected by clicking the Wrapping tab of the Format Text Box dialogue box shown on the next page. The default wrapping style is **In front of text**. To see what appears in our screen dump, click the **Tight** option, which also activates the **Wrap** text options in the dialogue box, with **Both sides** being the default.

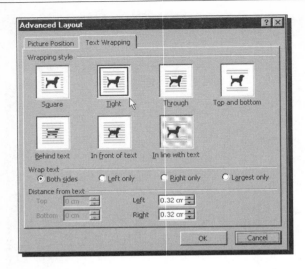

Once the suggested selections have been made on the Format Text Box, your document should look as follows:

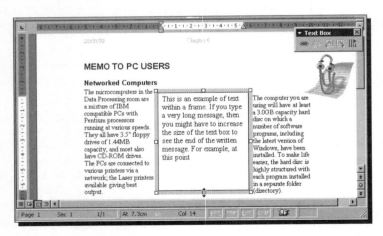

The small Text Box menu bar at the top right-hand side of the above display allows you to create and break forward text box links, to go to the previous and next text box, and change text direction.

Sizing Text Boxes

There are two ways of sizing text boxes; with the mouse, or with the keyboard using the Size tab on the Format Text Box.

Sizing a Text Box with the Mouse: To size a text box with the mouse, select it so that the square selection handles appear around the text box, then move the mouse pointer over one of the selection handles until it turns to the two-headed sizing arrow, as shown on the previous screen dump. Drag the sizing arrow to change the text box to the required size, then release the mouse button.

Dragging one of the corner handles will drag the two attached text box sides with the pointer, but dragging a centre line handle will only move that side. Try these actions until you are happy with the resultant text box.

Sizing a Text Box with the Keyboard: To size a text box with the keyboard, first select it, then use the **Format, Text Box** command which displays the Format Text Box dialogue box. In this box, click the Size tab, then specify the **Height** and **Width** of the required text box.

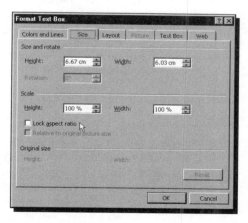

As you can see from this dialogue box, you also have other options available to you, including the ability to lock the aspect ratio of an imported graphic.

Rotating Text in a Text Box

Once you have your text box with its contents where you want it on the page, you can rotate it, using the **Change Text Direction** button on the Text Box bar, as shown below.

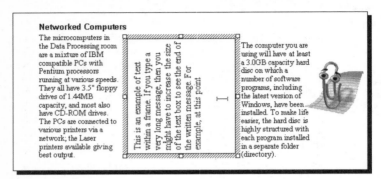

Next, click the mouse button outside the text box, which will cancel the text box selection; you will then not be able to access, or edit, the text inside it until you next click inside the text box. Finally, save this as **PC Users6**.

Moving the mouse pointer over the sides of the text box, turns it into a four-headed arrow, allowing you to move the text box to a new position when you click and drag. You can select the text box by single clicking which will let you re-size it, and if you clicked anywhere on the text within the text box, will also allow you to edit that text.

Importing a Picture

To import a graphic into a Word document, select the **Insert, Picture, Clip Art** command, which will open the Microsoft Clip Gallery dialogue box shown on the next page. This dialogue box allows you to select a category of Clip Art pictures which then displays various graphics held under this category. We selected Animals, then the cockerel, and clicked the **Insert clip** button, pointed to here, which brings the graphic into our document.

Pointing to the graphic and right-clicking displays a shortcut menu, the last option of which allows you to select the wrapping style, as discussed earlier.

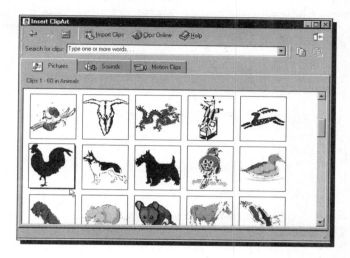

The display below shows the result of selecting the **Tight** option of wrapping. Pointing to the inserted graphic, changes the mouse pointer to a four-headed arrow which allows you to move the graphic to the required position. Note that the graphic was inserted in the document without the need for a containing frame, which allows for better wrapping around the graphic.

MEMO TO PC USERS

Networked Computers
The microcomputers in the Data Processing room are a mixture of IBM compatible PCs with Pentium processors running at various speeds. They all have 3.5" floppy drives of 1.44MB capacity, and most also have CD-ROM drives. The PCs are connected to various printers via a network; the Laser printers available giving best output.

The computer you are using will have at least a 3.0GB capacity hard disc on which a number of software programs, including the latest version of Windows, have been installed. To make life easier, the hard disc is highly structured with each program installed in a separate folder (directory).

Save this document under the filename **PC Users7**.

The Picture Bar

Should you want to change a picture you have inserted into your document, use the **<u>V</u>iew, <u>T</u>oolbars** command and select **Picture** from the drop-down menu. The tools on this bar can be used to manipulate pictures to suit your needs. Their functions are as follows:

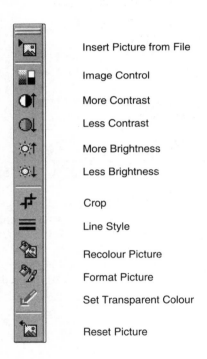

Insert Picture from File

Image Control

More Contrast

Less Contrast

More Brightness

Less Brightness

Crop

Line Style

Recolour Picture

Format Picture

Set Transparent Colour

Reset Picture

Try using these tools on the imported image to see how you can enhance or utterly destroy it! If, at the end of the day, you don't save it, it doesn't matter what you do to it. Just experiment.

The Drawing Tools

Should you want to create a drawing in your document, use the **View**, **Toolbars** command and select **Drawing** from the drop-down menu. You can use the Drawing tools to create, or edit, a graphic consisting of lines, arcs, ellipses, rectangles, and even text boxes. These can either exist in their own right, or be additions to a picture or object.

The various buttons on the Drawing toolbar have the following functions (see also next page):

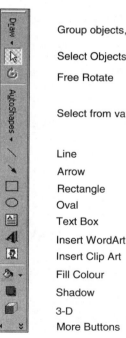

Group objects, etc.

Select Objects

Free Rotate

Select from various shapes

Line

Arrow

Rectangle

Oval

Text Box

Insert WordArt

Insert Clip Art

Fill Colour

Shadow

3-D

More Buttons

The Drawing Toolbar

The various functions offered by the Drawing Toolbar are shared by all Office 2000 applications and give Word a superior graphics capability. Amongst the many features available are:

AutoShapes – the additional AutoShape categories, such as connectors, block arrows, flowchart symbols, stars and banners, callouts, and action buttons make drawing diagrams much easier.

Bezier curves – used to easily create exact curves with pinpoint precision.

3-D effects – allow you to transform 2-D shapes into realistic 3-D objects with new 3-D effects, such as changing the lighting perspective of a 3-D object.

Perspective shadows – allow you to select from a wide range of shadows with perspective, and you can adjust the depth and angle of each shadow to make pictures more realistic.

Connectors – used to create diagrams and flowcharts with new straight, angled, and curved connectors between the shapes; when shapes are moved, the connectors remain attached and automatically reposition themselves.

Arrowhead styles – allow you to change the width and height of arrowheads for maximum effect.

Object alignment – allow you to distribute and space objects evenly, both horizontally and vertically.

Precise line-width control – allows you increased control over the width of lines by selecting pre-set options or customised line widths.

Image editing – lets you easily adjust the brightness or contrast of a picture.

Transparent background – allows you to insert a bitmap on your slides or Web pages so as to appear to be part of the design by turning background colours into transparent areas.

Creating a Drawing

The effects of the drawing tools can be superimposed either on the document area or on top of a graphic. The result is that you can annotate drawings and pictures to your total satisfaction.

To create an object, click on the required Drawing button, such as the **Oval** or **Rectangle**, position the mouse pointer where you want to create the object on the screen, and then drag the mouse to draw the object. Hold the <Shift> key while you drag the mouse to create a perfect circle or square. If you do not hold <Shift>, Word creates an oval or a rectangle.

You can use the **AutoShapes** button to select from a variety of pre-drawn **Lines**, **Basic Shapes**, etc. First click on the desired line or shape, then position the mouse pointer where you want to create the object on the screen and click the left mouse button to fix it on that position.

Editing a Drawing

To select an object, click on it. Word displays white handles around the object selected.

You can move an object, or multiple objects, within a draw area by selecting them and dragging to the desired position. To copy an object, click at the object, then use the **Edit, Copy** / **Edit, Paste** commands.

To size an object, position the mouse pointer on a white handle and then drag the handle until the object is the desired shape and size.

To delete an object, select it and press the <Del> key. To delete a drawing, hold the <Shift> key down and click each object in turn that makes up the drawing, unless they are grouped or framed, then press <Del>.

Do try out some of these commands using the **PC Users7** document file, but do not save the results of your experimentation under the same file name.

Using Layered Drawings

You can right-click an object, select the **Order** option from the displayed shortcut menu, then use the **Bring to Front** or **Send to Back** sub-menu options to determine the order of layered drawings. Drawings, or pictures, layered on top of each other can create useful visual effects, provided you remember that the top drawing and/or picture obscures the one below it, as shown below.

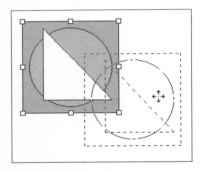

Here we have used Draw's Rectangle, Oval, and the AutoShapes, Right Angle options to draw the three displayed shapes. The order you draw these is not important as you can use the Bring to Front and Send to Back options to rearrange them to your taste. We then selected each shape in turn, and used the Fill Color button to give them different shades from the displayed options to the right.

Finally, we selected each shape, while holding down the <Shift> key, then used the **Draw** button and clicked **Group** from the displayed menu to lock them together, before attempting to move the whole group down and to the right (you can tell they are grouped because attempting to move them, moves the whole group, shown above in a dotted outline).

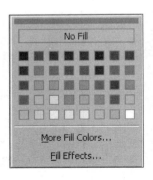

Do experiment with these and other options, and when satisfied with the result of your efforts, save your work under the filename **PC Users8**.

Inserting Objects into a Document

You can insert an Object into a document by using the **Insert, Object** command which causes the following dialogue box to appear on your screen:

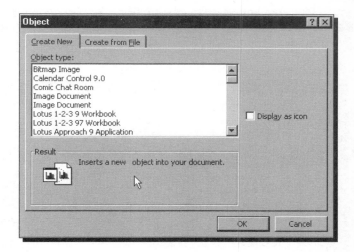

From here, you can choose different 'Object types', from a Lotus 1-2-3 Worksheet to a WordPad Document. For example, if you select 'Microsoft Equation 3.0' from the **Object type** list, Word displays the Equation Editor shown below.

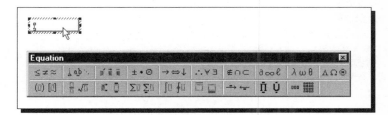

This allows you to build mathematical equations which can then be included in your Word document.

Inserting an Equation

If building equations is not your cup of tea, you can safely skip this section. If, on the other hand, you want to learn to build equations, activate the Equation Editor and press **F1** to display the following Help screen. Selecting the first option, reveals a further list of topics under it, as shown below, of which the most important to look up first are: 'Equation Editor Basics' and 'Equation Editor, and what it can do'. The first tells you about the Equation Toolbar and how you can use it.

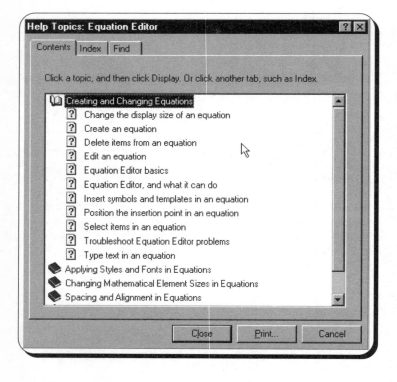

For example, the top row of the Equation Editor toolbar has buttons for inserting more than 150 mathematical symbols, many of which are not available in the standard Symbol font.

To insert a symbol in an equation, click a button on the top row of the toolbar, as shown on the composite screen dump below, and then click the specific symbol from the palette that appears under the button.

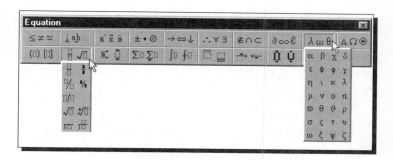

The bottom row of the Equation Editor toolbar has buttons for inserting templates or frameworks that contain such symbols as fractions, radicals, summations, integrals, products, matrices, and various fences or matching pairs of symbols such as brackets and braces. There are about 120 templates, grouped on palettes, many of which contain slots - spaces into which you type text and insert symbols. Templates can be nested, by inserting them in the slots of other templates, to build complex hierarchical formulae.

Finally, select the second recommended help topic to find out about spacing and alignment, expanding templates, styles, embellishments, and how to position the insertion pointer so that you can achieve best results.

As an example, we will take you through the steps required, when using the Equation Editor, to construct the equation for the solution of a quadratic equation. The required equation is shown overleaf.

$$x = \frac{-b \pm \sqrt{\left\{b^2 - 4ac\right\}}}{2a}$$

To construct this equation, place the insertion pointer at the required place in your document, activate the Equation Editor, and follow the steps listed below. The templates and symbols you require from the Equation Editor are shown to the right of the appropriate step.

- Type *x =* followed by selecting the template shown here from the lower second button.

- Type *–b* followed by selecting the ± symbol from the upper fourth button.

- Select the square root template shown here from the lower second button.

- Select the brackets template shown here from the lower first button.

- Type *b* followed by selecting the template from the lower third button.

- Type **2** and re-position the insertion pointer as shown here, and then type *–4ac*.

- Position the insertion pointer at the denominator and type **2a**.

Obviously, the Equation Editor is capable of a lot more than what we have covered here, but this simple example should serve to get you started. Try it, it's simpler than it looks.

7

Using Tables and Graphs

The ability to use 'Tables' is built into most top-range word processors these days. At first glance the process might look complicated and perhaps only a small percentage of users take advantage of the facility, which is a pity because using a 'Table' has many possibilities. If you have worked with a spreadsheet, such as Excel or Lotus 1-2-3, then you are familiar with tables.

Tables are used to create adjacent columns of text and numeric data. A table is simply a grid of columns and rows with the intersection of a column and row forming a rectangular box which is referred to as a 'cell'. In Word you can include pictures, charts, notes, footnotes, tabs, and page breaks in your tables. There are several ways to place information into a table:

- Type the desired text, or numeric data.

- Paste text from the main document.

- Link two tables within a document.

- Insert data created in another application.

- Import a picture.

- Create a chart on information held in a table.

The data is placed into individual cells that are organised into columns and rows, similar to a spreadsheet. You can modify the appearance of table data by applying text formatting and enhancements, or by using different paragraph styles.

Creating a Table

Tables can be created either by pressing the 'Insert Table'

button on the toolbar, shown here, or by using the **Table, Insert, Table** command. Using the latter method, displays the dialogue box shown to the

right, which enables you to size the column widths at that point.

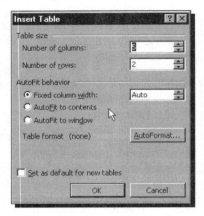

As an example we will step through the process of creating the table shown on page 126. Open a 'New' file (it could be an existing file, in which case you place the insertion point where you want the table to appear), then click on the 'Table' button and drag down and to the right.

As you drag the mouse, the 'Table' button expands to

10 x 5 Table

create the grid of rows and columns. At the bottom of the box there is an automatic display of the number of rows and columns you are selecting by this method. When you release the mouse button, a table is inserted in your document the size of the selected grid.

For our example, we require a 10x5 cell table. Once this appears in position, the cursor is placed in the top left cell awaiting your input. The cells forming the table, are displayed with lines around each cell. To move around in a table, simply click the desired cell, or use one of the keyboard commands listed on the next page.

Navigating with the Keyboard

To navigate around a table when using the keyboard, use the following keys:

Press this	To do this
Tab	Moves the insertion point right one cell, in the same row, and from the last cell in one row to the first cell in the next row. If the cell contains information it highlights the contents.
Shift+Tab	Moves the insertion point left one cell. If the cell contains information it highlights the contents.
↑,↓,←, and →	Moves the insertion point within cells, between cells, and between the cells in a table and the main document text.
Home	Moves the insertion point to the beginning of the current line within a cell.
Alt+Home	Moves the insertion point to the first column in the current row.
End	Moves the insertion point to the end of the current line within a cell.
Alt+End	Moves the insertion point to the last column in the current row.
Alt+PgUp	Moves the insertion point to the top cell in the column.
Alt+PgDn	Moves the insertion point to the bottom cell in the column.

Now type in the information given below and format your table using the buttons on the Formatting Toolbar to align the contents of the various cells as shown.

Types of Removable Discs				
Description	Capacity Kbytes	Price/Unit Pence	Number Bought	Cost in £
Double-density diskettes	720	30	60	
High-density diskettes	1,440	40	80	
Removable Zip discs	100,000	500	6	
Removable Zip discs	250,000	1,300	4	
Removable hard discs	1,500,000	5,800	1	
			Total	

To enter the heading as shown, highlight all the columns of the first row, then use the **Table, Merge Cells** command to join all the cells into one. Now you can type the heading, centre it, format it in bold, and increase its font size to your liking.

The line in the cell of the penultimate row and last column was typed by using the **Insert, Symbol** command, and selecting a line character from the Symbol font that fills the entire width of the character. Inserting this character repeatedly, gives the impression of a continuous horizontal line.

Changing Column Width and Row Height

The column width of selected cells or entire columns can be changed by dragging the table column markers on the ruler or by dragging the column boundaries, as shown in the adjacent display.

Description	Capacity Kbytes

You can also drag a column boundary while holding down other keys. The overall effects of these actions are listed on the next page.

Keys	Effect
No key	Only the columns to the left and right are re-sized proportionally with the overall width of the table remaining the same size.
Shift key	Only the column to the left is re-sized with the overall width of the table changing by the same amount.
Ctrl key	As the column to the left changes, all columns to the right change proportionally, but the overall width of the table remains the same.

The height of a row depends on its contents. As you type text into a cell, its height increases to accommodate it. You can also increase the height of a cell by inserting empty lines before or after the text by pressing the <Enter> key. All other cells in that row become the same height as the largest cell. In Word 2000, you can also increase the height of rows by dragging a row boundary down.

The width of a column and the height of a row can also be changed by using the **Table, Table Properties** command to display a dialogue box with appropriate tabs for controlling size and the placement of a table, the column and row size, as well as the alignment of entries within cells.

When you have finished, save your work under the filename **Table 1**. We will use this table to show you how you can insert expressions into cells to make your table behave just like a spreadsheet.

Entering Expressions

To enter an expression into a table cell, so that you can carry out spreadsheet type calculations, select the cell and use the **Table, Formula** command which displays the dialogue box shown on the next page. Word automatically analyses the table and suggests an appropriate formula in the **Formula** box of the displayed dialogue box, as shown.

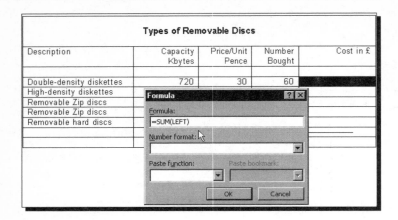

In the above situation, it has found numbers in cells to the left of the highlighted cell, therefore it suggests the SUM(LEFT) formula. To replace this formula, simply delete it from the **Formula** box and type the new formula preceded by the equal (=) sign.

For example, to calculate the cost of purchased discs in Sterling (£) in cell E4, type the following formula in the **Formula** box:

```
=C4*D4/100
```

Word performs mathematical calculations on numbers in cells and inserts the result of the calculation as a field in the cell that contains the insertion pointer. Cells are referred to

as A1, A2, B1, B2, and so on, with the letter representing a column and the number representing a row. Thus, B3 refers to the hatched cell.

When you use the **Table, Formula** command, Word assumes addition, unless you indicate otherwise, and proposes a sum based on the following rules:

- If the cell that contains the insertion pointer is at the intersection of a row and column and both contain numbers, Word sums the column. To sum the row, type =SUM(LEFT) or =SUM(RIGHT) in the **Formula** box, depending on the location of the insertion pointer.

- If the cell that contains the insertion pointer contains text or numbers, they are ignored.

- Word evaluates numbers beginning with the cell closest to the cell that contains the insertion pointer and continues until it reaches either a blank cell or a cell that contains text.

- If the numbers you are calculating include a number format, such as a £ sign, the result will also contain that format.

Fill in the rest of column E (unfortunately you will have to retype the formula in each cell as there is no apparent method of replication), then to calculate the total cost, place the insertion pointer in cell E9 and use the **Table, Formula** command. Word analyses your table and suggests the following function:

```
=SUM(ABOVE)
```

which is the correct formula in this case. On pressing **OK**, Word calculates the result and places it in cell E9. The completed table should look as follows:

Types of Removable Discs				
Description	Capacity Kbytes	Price/Unit Pence	Number Bought	Cost in £
Double-density diskettes	720	30	60	18
High-density diskettes	1,440	40	80	32
Removable Zip discs	100,000	500	6	30
Removable Zip discs	250,000	1,300	4	52
Removable hard discs	1,500,000	5,800	1	58
			Total	190

As the result of a calculation is inserted as a field in the cell that contains the insertion pointer, if you change the contents of the referenced cells, you must update the calculation. To do this, select the field (the cell that contains the formula) by highlighting it and press the **F9** function key.

In a formula you can specify any combination of mathematical and logical operators from the following list.

Addition	+
Subtraction	−
Multiplication	*
Division	/
Percent	%
Powers and roots	^
Equal to	=
Less than	<
Less than or equal to	<=
Greater than	>
Greater than or equal to	>=
Not equal to	< >

The functions below accept references to table cells:

ABS( )	AND( )	AVERAGE( )
COUNT( )	DEFINED( )	FALSE( )
IF( )	INT( )	MAX( )
MIN( )	MOD( )	NOT( )
OR( )	PRODUCT( )	ROUND( )
SIGN( )	SUM( )	TRUE( )

The main reason for using formulae in a table, instead of just typing in the numbers, is that formulae will still give the correct final answer even if some of the data is changed. However, you must remember to update the formulae fields of the affected cells by pressing **F9**.

Editing a Table

You can edit a table by inserting or deleting columns or rows, or by merging or splitting cells, as follows:

To insert a column or row: Select the cell where you want

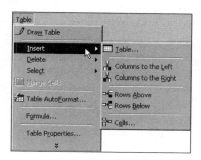

the new row or column to appear, then use the **Table**, **Insert** command and choose an appropriate option from the drop-down menu shown here. This version of Word, allows you to insert columns or rows to either side of the selected cell. You can even insert a single cell.

To delete a cell, a column or row: Select the cell whose

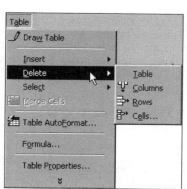

column or row you want to delete, then use the **Table**, **Delete** command and choose an appropriate option from the drop-down menu shown here. As you can see from the available options, you can even delete a single cell or an entire table.

To merge cells: Select the cells you want to merge, then use the **Table**, **Merge Cells** command.

To split cells: Move the insertion pointer to the cell you want to split, then use the **Table**, **Split Cells** command. The adjacent dialogue box is displayed which can be used to subdivide a cell.

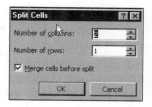

To split a table: To split a table, click the row that you want to be the first row of the second table and select the **Table, Split Table** command. Using this command on the first row of a table, allows you to insert text before a table. In the example below, the insertion pointer was placed in the second row before splitting the table.

Types of Removable Discs				
Description	Capacity Kbytes	Price/Unit Pence	Number Bought	Cost in £
Double-density diskettes	720	30	60	18
High-density diskettes	1,440	40	80	32
Removable Zip discs	100,000	500	6	30
Removable Zip discs	250,000	1,300	4	52
Removable hard discs	1,500,000	5,800	1	58
			Total	190

To learn more about tables, place the insertion pointer inside a table, activate the Assistant, request information on 'working with tables', and select the first item on the returned list entitled 'About tables'. This option opens the Microsoft Word Help screen, which contains a wealth of information, the first part of which is shown below.

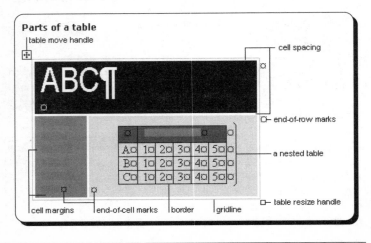

Formatting a Table

You can enhance the looks of a table by selecting one of several pre-defined styles. As an example, open the previously saved version of **Table 2**, place the insertion pointer in a cell in the table and use the **Ta̲ble, Table AutoF̲ormat** command. The following dialogue box appears on your screen:

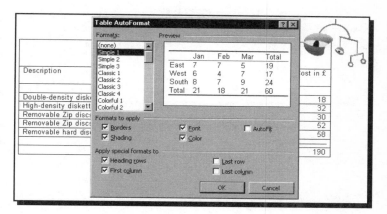

Select Simple 3 from the **Format̲s** list, to produce the following professional looking table.

Types of Removable Discs				
Description	Capacity Kbytes	Price/Unit Pence	Number Bought	Cost in £
Double-density diskettes	720	30	60	18
High-density diskettes	1,440	40	80	32
Removable Zip discs	100,000	500	6	30
Removable Zip discs	250,000	1,300	4	52
Removable hard discs	1,500,000	5,800	1	58
			Total	190

Finally, save the result of this formatting as **Table 3**.

Using Microsoft Graph

To chart your Word data, you can use Microsoft Graph 2000, which can be activated by using the **Insert, Object** command and selecting 'Microsoft Graph 2000 Chart' from the list in the Object dialogue box, shown below:

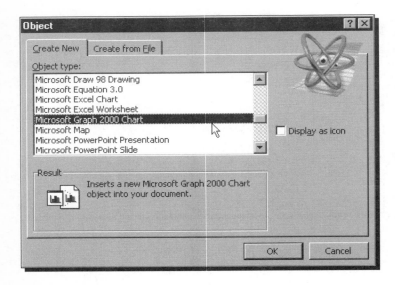

Pressing the **OK** button displays the following screen, provided no table was selected in your document.

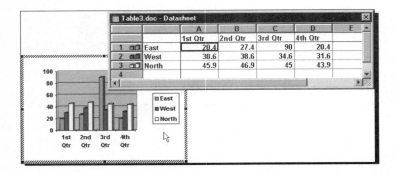

This is an internal Word example, showing the capabilities of the package. To demonstrate the way in which you can chart data held in a Word table, open **Table 2** and then use your editing skills to transform it to what is displayed below.

Removable Discs	Price/Unit Pence	Number Bought	Cost in £
Double-density diskettes	30	60	18
High-density diskettes	40	80	32
Removable Zip discs	150	6	30
Removable Zip discs	300	4	52

Note that we have replaced 'Description' with 'Removable Discs', and changed the per unit price of the Zip discs (we managed to find a cheaper supplier, if only!) - actually we needed to limit the range of the numbers within this column so that the chart would be better balanced. Also, we have deleted the column dealing with 'Capacity Kbytes' and the row dealing with the removable hard discs (for the same charting limitations), as well as the empty row below the column headings.

Save the resultant work as **Table 4**. Then select the table, by either using the **Table, Select Table** command, or highlighting it as shown below.

Removable Discs	Price/Unit Pence	Number Bought	Cost in £
Double-density diskettes	30	60	18
High-density diskettes	40	80	32
Removable Zip discs	150	6	30
Removable Zip discs	300	4	52

Next, and while the table is selected, activate Microsoft Graph 2000 by using the **Insert, Object** command and selecting 'Microsoft Graph 2000 Chart' from the list in the displayed Object dialogue box (see previous page). Microsoft Graph 2000 displays the following table and chart.

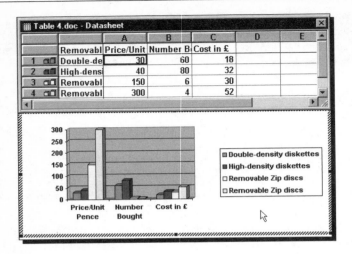

When you click outside the graph area, the chart is embedded in your Word document. To edit such a chart, double-click the chart area to display the Datasheet shown above. When the Datasheet is activated, the menu bar option **Ta̱ble** is replaced by two other options, **Data** and **C̱hart**. The respective sub-menus for these two are shown below.

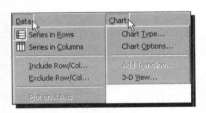

To display the captions in the first column of your table as the x-axis labels and those of the first row as the legends, use the **Data, Series by C̱olumns** command. This displays the following screen:

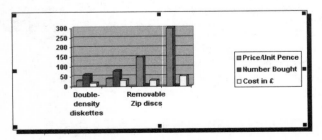

Pre-defined Chart Types

To select a different type of chart, use the **Chart, Chart Type** command which opens the dialogue box below.

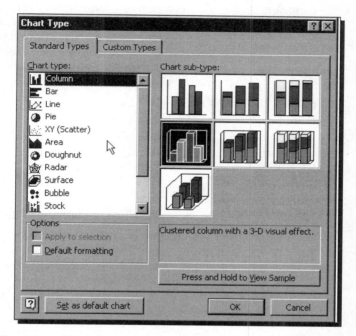

The Chart Type dialogue box lists 14 different chart options. These chart-types are normally used to describe the following relationships between data:

 Area: for showing a volume relationship between two series, such as production or sales, over a given length of time.

 Bar: for comparing differences in non-continuous data that are not related over time, by depicting changes in horizontal bars to show positive and negative variations from a given position.

Bubble: for showing a type of XY (scatter) chart. The size of the data (radius of the bubble) indicates the value of a third variable.

Column: for comparing separate items (non-continuous data which are related over time) by depicting changes in vertical bars to show positive and negative variations from a given position.

Cone: for showing 3-D column and bar charts in a more dramatic way.

Cylinder: similar to Cone.

Doughnut: for comparing parts with the whole. Similar to pie charts, but can depict more than one series of data.

Line: for showing continuous changes in data with time.

Pie: for comparing parts with the whole. You can use this type of chart when you want to compare the percentage of an item from a single series of data with the whole series.

Pyramid: similar to Cone.

Radar: for plotting one series of data as angle values defined in radians, against one or more series defined in terms of a radius.

Surface: for showing optimum combinations between two sets of data, as in a topographic map. Colours and patterns indicate areas that are in the same range of values.

Stock: for showing high-low-close type of data variation to illustrate stock market prices or temperature changes.

 XY (Scatter): for showing scatter relationships between X and Y. Scatter charts are used to depict items which are not related over time.

You can change the type of chart by selecting one of the fourteen alternate chart types from the Chart Type dialogue box, provided your data fits the selection. To preview your choice, select one **Chart sub-type** and press the **Press and Hold to View Sample** button on the dialogue box.

Clicking the Custom Types tab of the Chart Type dialogue box, reveals additional choices within the 14 main types of charts. For example, you can choose between several types of charts either in colour or in black and white, charts with logarithmic scale, or charts depicted as stacks of colours or even tubes.

Improving a Microsoft Chart

A Microsoft Chart can be improved by using the Microsoft Draw facility (to activate it use the **View, Toolbars** command and click Drawing). We have used the Arrow and Text Box buttons on the Drawing Toolbar to point to and annotate the 'Best Buy' on the chart shown below, and give it a title. As each value in the data used to create the chart is a separate object, it can be moved, changed, or formatted.

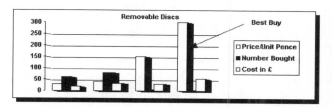

For example, double-clicking the chart title, then using the **Format, Text Box** command, displays the dialogue box shown on the next page.

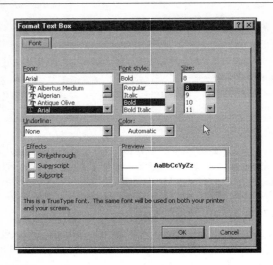

From here, you can change the Font, Alignment, Colours and Lines, Size, Properties, and Margins of the selected text box.

To further demonstrate some of the formatting capabilities of Microsoft Chart, we used the Drawing facility to add a title to the 'Best Buy' data, then used the **Format, Text Box** command and changed the Font colour to white, then clicked the Alignment tab and selected a vertical orientation, as shown below.

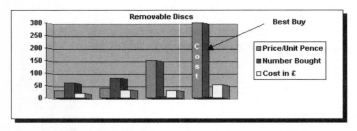

When you have carried out all the required changes to your chart, save the Word document as **Table 5**.

We are sure that you will get many hours of fun with the various features of Microsoft Graph and, more to the point, produce some very professional graphics for your reports.

8

Managing Large Documents

Many users' needs might demand that they work with either large documents, or with documents which are split into many files; they might also have to automate certain routines. In such cases, knowing something about outlines, file management and the design of macros is imperative.

Outline Mode

Outline mode provides a way of viewing and organising the contents of a document. Nine outline levels can be used and these could be based on formatted headings (Heading 1, Heading 2, through to Heading 7), plus Normal text. By assigning each heading level a different paragraph style, it allows easy assimilation of the contents of a document.

The following display shows part of the first page of Chapter 1 of this book in the Normal editing view.

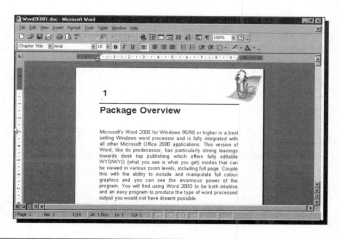

The same chapter is shown below in outline view obtained by either pressing the Outline button on the scroll bar, or selecting the **View, Outline** command. However, before you can see exactly what is shown here, you must assign styles to the various Headings. This can be done by selecting the outline view and assigning heading levels to your work using the tools on the outline bar which replaces the ruler.

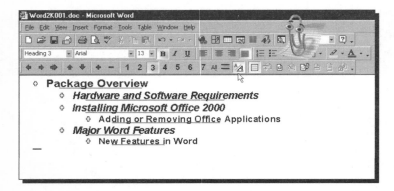

The actual formatting can only be seen if the Show Formatting icon (the one pointed to) is clicked.

Assigning Outline Levels

'Outline' levels are stored as part of the formatting information in the paragraph styles, so you must assign these levels to your paragraph styles before you can usefully use the 'Outline' mode. Then your outline will automatically display your document headings at the correct levels. This is an easy process carried out by selecting an existing heading and clicking one of the following buttons in the outline bar (shown below in two tiers):

The name and function of these buttons is listed below.

Buttons	Name	Function
←	**Promote**	Assigns heading to a higher outline level.
→	**Demote**	Assigns to a lower outline level.
⇒	**Double Arrow**	Demotes a heading to body text.
↑	**Move Up**	Moves selected text before the paragraph preceding it.
↓	**Move Down**	Moves selected text after the paragraph following it.
+	**Plus**	Displays hidden subordinate headings until text is reached.
−	**Minus**	Hides displayed subordinate text or lower level headings.
1 to 7		Displays all headings and text to the lowest selected level.
All	**Display All**	Displays all text if some is collapsed, else displays headings if all text is expanded.
=	**Display First Line**	Displays all body text, or just first line.
AA	**Show Formatting**	Shows or hides character formatting.
▤	**Master Doc View**	Displays Document in Master View.

Using the expand and collapse commands, you can display the entire document or only selected text. Editing a document in 'Outline' mode is simple because you can control the level of detail that displays and quickly see the structure of the document. If you want to focus on the main topics in the document, you can collapse the text to display only paragraph styles set to high outline levels. If you want to view additional detail, you can expand the text to display text using paragraph styles set to lower outline levels.

The other buttons on the Outline toolbar perform the following functions:

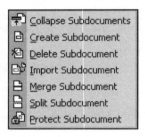

Outline Buttons

Another feature of the 'Outline' mode is the buttons placed before each paragraph. These not only show the status of the paragraph, but can be used to quickly manipulate paragraph text. The buttons placed before each paragraph have the following meaning:

∓   **Plus button** - Indicates that the paragraph is using a paragraph style set to an outline level between 1 and 7 and that the paragraph has subordinate text.

−   **Minus button** - Indicates that the paragraph is using a paragraph style set to an outline level between 1 and 7 and that the paragraph does not have any subordinate text.

□   **Box button** - Indicates that the paragraph is using a paragraph style set to an outline level of Normal text.

To display, or hide, subordinate text double-click a 'Plus' button. Click on a 'Plus' button and drag it, to move text to a new location. Word automatically moves the text as you drag the mouse. If you print from 'Outline' mode only the level of text that is seen on the screen will actually print.

Outline Numbering

If you want all your paragraphs numbered, you must rank all the styles, highlight all the paragraphs you want to number, and then assign one of the numbering schemes in the dialogue box obtained with the **Format, Bullets and Numbering** command. Click the **Numbered** tab, or if you want to modify the numbering system click the **Outline Numbered** tab, to obtain the dialogue box shown below.

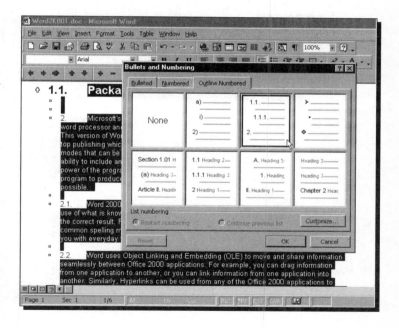

You could, of course, select the **Bulleted** tab, if you prefer.

Creating a Table of Contents or an Index

To create a table of contents, undo the Numbered option, return to Page Layout and position the insertion point where you want the table of contents to appear. Next, use the **Insert, Index and Tables** command, and click the **Table of Contents** tab to display the dialogue box below.

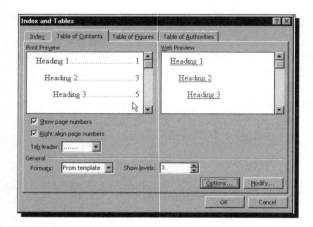

Pressing **OK** forms the table of contents shown below.

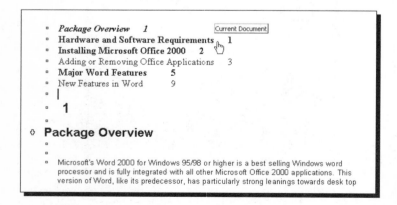

The above screen is in Outline view. To see the page numbers right-aligned with tab leaders, switch to Print view.

Also, note that each line in the Table of Contents is now a hyperlink to the corresponding heading in the document.

Before you can create an index, you must first mark all the text you want to appear in the index by highlighting it, before using the **Insert, Index and Tables** command which displays the Index and Tables dialogue box, shown below.

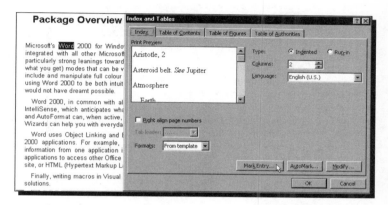

Next, press the **Index** tab, followed by the **Mark Entry** button which displays the Mark Index Entry dialogue box below.

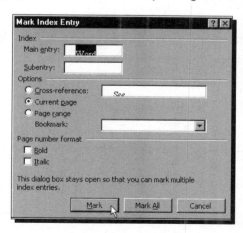

This can be quite a time consuming procedure, especially for a long document.

File Management

You can manage your documents from the **Open** menu option. First, you locate the drive and folder in which your file is to be found - you can use the buttons displayed at the top of the Open dialogue box, shown annotated below.

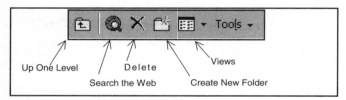

Up One Level   Delete   Views
        Search the Web   Create New Folder

The **Tools** button above, provides additional options for working with files. When the file is found (you can even use wildcard characters in the **File name** box), select it then right-click it to display the shortcut menu shown below. This contains all the commands you should ever need to manage your documents.

If more than one file is found, the first file is normally highlighted. If you click the **Views** button, pointed to below, full details on the listed files are displayed.

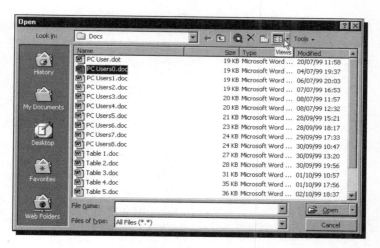

Pressing the **Views** button once more, displays information relating to the properties of the selected document.

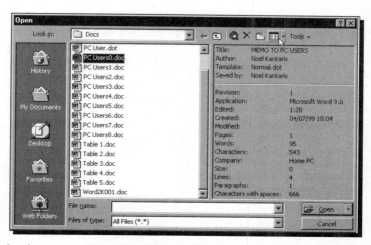

In fact, pressing the **Views** button successively, rotates through four different displays.

These options can also be selected from the **Views** drop-down menu shown below. For example, selecting the **Pre<u>v</u>iew** option, displays the selected document in the Preview box. As you select another file from the list, Word displays its contents too.

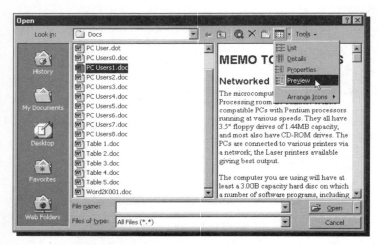

The order of the files displayed in the List box can be changed by selecting the **Arrange <u>I</u>cons** option from the **Views** menu, and choosing a preferred list order.

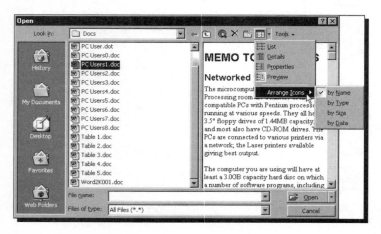

Assembling a Master Document

If you are involved in writing long documents, such as books, it is sometimes best if you split each document into sections (or chapters) of approximately 20 pages long. Anything above this length, particularly if it contains graphics, will strain your computer's resources. How much strain is experienced depends on how fast your computer is and how much Random Access Memory (RAM) it contains. In any case, large files take longer to open and save.

If you have broken a long document into smaller files you can work with these separately until you need to print your work in its entirety, or create a table of contents and an index with the page numbers. You will then need to create a 'Master Document'.

One method of doing this is to open a new document in Word, then use the **View, Outline** command which displays the Outlining toolbar. Next, press the 'Insert Subdocument' button on this toolbar, shown to the left and pointed to below, then locate and select the file you want to insert into your Master Document from those listed in the Open dialogue box.

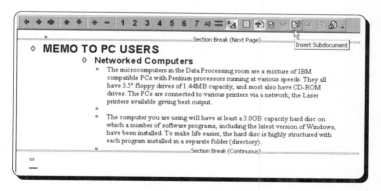

The selected document is then inserted by Word in your Master Document and the insertion pointer is moved below the Section Break waiting for more sub-documents to be inserted.

Printing a Master Document

When you are finally ready to print the Master Document to paper, you can either print the entire document or specify the amount of detail you want to print.

To print the entire Master Document, expand the sub-documents, then switch to Normal view and print as usual. To specify the amount of detail you want to print, display the Master Document in Outline view, expand or collapse headings to display as much of the document as you require, then use the **File**, **Print** command.

9

E-mail and Hyperlinks

This latest version of Microsoft Word has many design features built around the Internet, the main ones being its use as an e-mail editor and its ability to create and customise Web pages. Both of these features rely to a large extent on the new ability to save any Word document as a fully editable HTML file.

HTML File Format

Most Web pages are written in HTML (Hypertext Markup Language), which can be used by Web browsers on any operating system, such as Windows, Macintosh, and UNIX.

HTML pages are actually text documents which use short codes, or tags, to control text, designate graphical elements and hypertext links. Clicking a link on a Web page brings a document located on your hard disc, a local Intranet, or on a distant Internet server to your screen, irrespective of the server's geographic location. Documents may contain text, images, sounds, movies, or a combination of these, in other words - multimedia. All of these are 'built into' a Web page with HTML code.

E-mails created in Word 2000 use the HTML format. Most Windows application programs save their files, or data documents, in a proprietary binary format, which can only be read by the program itself. Word 2000, like earlier versions of Word, uses the .doc file format as the 'main' file saving format. Word documents can now, however, be saved in HTML as an alternative file format, and the document can still be updated and edited using all of Word's extensive formatting tools.

This means that not only can Word 2000 documents now be published as 'instant' Web pages, but they can also be sent to other people, in a workgroup for example, who can read them in their Web browsers if they don't have a copy of Word 2000 on their computer. Office 2000 is in fact making HTML into a 'universal' file format, its application files being instantly readable by anyone with a normal Web browser.

To do this, extensive use is made of 'style sheets', and the downside is that the actual HTML code produced by Word is far too complex and convoluted for most Web authors to edit manually. Our example below shows only a quarter of the code produced for a document of only four lines of text. HTML documents produced this way can only really be edited in the original application itself.

```
p.MsoBodyText, li.MsoBodyText, div.MsoBodyText { mso-pagination: widow-orphan; f
                font-family: Times New Roman; mso-fareast-font-family:
                Times New Roman; margin-left: 0cm; margin-right: 0cm;
                margin-top: 0cm; margin-bottom: .0001pt }
@page Section1
    {size:612.0pt 792.0pt;
    margin:72.0pt 90.0pt 72.0pt 90.0pt;
    mso-header-margin:36.0pt;
    mso-footer-margin:36.0pt;
    mso-paper-source:0;}
div.Section1 { page: Section1 }
-->
</style>
</head>

<body lang="EN-GB" style="tab-interval:36.0pt">

<div class="Section1">
  <p class="MsoBodyText"><b><i><span style="font-size:20.0pt;mso-bidi-font-size:
10.0pt">The Seagull<o:p></o:p></span></i></b></p>
  <p class="MsoBodyText"><span style="font-size:14.0pt;mso-bidi-font-size:10.0pt'
    seagull lies dead near the breaking waves.<b> </b>Stranded in death on the
    rocks and pebbles that lay strewn on the beach, each one appearing to me as a
    jewel of exquisite beauty.<span style="mso-spacerun: yes">  </span>The
    red coloured seaweed near the bird's head like a bloodstained pillow for its
    downy head. <o:p></o:p></span></p>
  <p class="MsoNormal"><![if !supportEmptyParas]> <![endif]><o:p></o:p></p>
</div>
<div style="mso-element:comment-list">
  <![if !supportAnnotations]>

  <hr class="msocomoff" align="left" size="1" width="33%">

  <![endif]>
</div>

</body>

</html>
```

E-mail

E-mail, or electronic mail, has to be one of the main uses of the Internet. It is very much faster that letter mail, known as 'snailmail' by many e-mail users. It consists of electronic text, that can be transmitted, sometimes in seconds, to anywhere else in the World that is connected to a main network. E-mail can also be used to send software and data files by attaching the files to a message.

There are many software packages dedicated to reading and sending e-mails, and we have probably tried most of them. Our version of Office 2000 came bundled with Outlook 2000, Microsoft's latest e-mail and news editor. We find this an excellent program, especially as you can use Word to perform all the writing and editing of your e-mails. For more detail of using this package we suggest you try our book *Microsoft Office 2000 explained* (BP471), also published by Bernard Babani (publishing) Ltd. In what follows we assume you have installed Outlook and have it set up with the details of your e-mail Internet account.

Word and Outlook 2000

If you use Outlook 2000 as your default mail client, you can use Word 2000 as your e-mail editor, instead of Outlook's much less powerful one. You can then create and edit your messages in Word using its extra features such as, automatic spelling, grammar checking, AutoCorrect, tables, the Document Map view, and the automatic conversion of e-mail names and Internet addresses into hyperlinks.

Configuring Outlook for E-mail

To configure Outlook 2000 to send and receive e-mail, open the program and use the **Tools**, **Accounts** menu command to open the dialogue box shown on the next page.

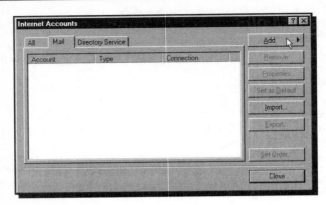

With the Mail tab pressed, click the **Add** button and select **Mail** from the displayed menu to start the Internet Connection Wizard which asks you in successive screens to:

* Type in your name and your e-mail address. This is supplied to you by your Internet Service Provider, or ISP, when you join their services.

* Specify the type of your incoming mail server, usually POP3, then type in the name of the 'Incoming' and 'Outgoing' mail server. This information is also supplied to you by your ISP.

* Type in your 'account name' and 'password' - again supplied to you by your ISP.

* Click the **Connect using my phone line** radio button (if that is how you are connected to the Internet), and select your ISP for your Dial-Up Networking connection.

If all is well, the final 'Congratulations' screen appears and the Wizard places an additional **Send/Receive** button on the Outlook toolbar, as shown below.

Unless you have Outlook 2000 configured as your default
e-mail program many of the e-mail features of Word 2000 will

not work. A quick way to check this, is to look at the
E-mail button on the standard Word toolbar. If it is
not 'active' and does not light up when you move the
pointer over it, you should use the following
procedure to set Outlook as your default e-mail program.

Click the Windows **Start** menu, followed by **Settings**, and
Control Panel, then double-click on Internet Options to open
the Internet Properties dialogue box shown here.

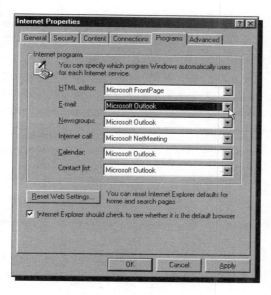

Open the **Programs** page and select Microsoft Outlook from
the drop-down list in the **E-mail** box. Clicking **OK** will confirm
the new setting, but you will have to re-start your PC for the
change to actually take effect.

There is one other setting that may also need changing to
fully benefit from Word and its e-mail facilities. Open Outlook
2000, action the **Tools**, **Options** menu command, click the
Mail Format tab and make sure that the **Use Microsoft
Word to edit e-mail messages** option is selected.

E-mailing a Document

There are often times when we are creating documents in Word when we reach the stage that we want to send it to someone else, maybe for comment, or approval. This is now very easy to do straight from Word 2000 itself. With the

document open in Word, you simply click the E-mail button, or use the **File**, **Send To**, **Mail Recipient** command sequence. These both open the e-mail header, shown below, in which you control the e-mail posting.

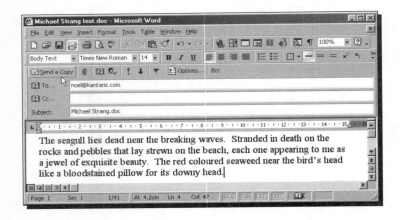

Typing the e-mail address of your recipient in the **To** box and clicking the **Send a Copy** button is all you need to do. This actually sends the document to Outlook's Outbox. When it is actually transmitted will depend on your type of connection and the settings in Outlook's **Tools**, **Options** dialogue box. We have our 'Mail account options', located on the **Mail Delivery** page, set to **Send messages immediately when connected**. With this setting, all our messages are sent whenever we are actually connected to our ISP. When we are not connected they are stored in the Outbox. If we had a 'permanent', or Local Area Network, connection to the Internet, our messages would be transmitted straight away.

When you e-mail a document in this way, Word sends a copy of the document in HTML format, and then closes the e-mail header. The original document, however, stays open so that you can continue working on it if you want. When you save the document, the e-mail 'send' information is also saved with the document. The next time you e-mail a copy of this document, the e-mail information appears in the e-mail header, as shown here, making it easy to send further updates to the same recipients.

Sending E-mail Messages

If you have set up to use Word as your e-mail editor, as described earlier, you still use Outlook to read your incoming messages, but whenever you click Outlook's **New** toolbar button to start a new e-mail message, a new Word window with the e-mail header bar, shown here, will open for you.

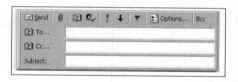

To start a new e-mail message straight from Word 2000, either click the **E-mail** button on the standard toolbar, or use the **File**, **New** menu command, click the **General** tab, and then double-click the 'E-mail Message' icon shown on the next page.

If the above icon is not in the New dialogue box, it is probably because you have not set Outlook 2000 as your default e-mail program, as described earlier in the chapter.

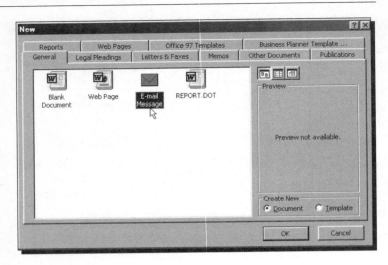

In the Word window that opens, you type the recipient's e-mail address in the **To** box, a title in the **Subject** box, and type your message, letter, memo, etc., in the main area, as shown in our example below.

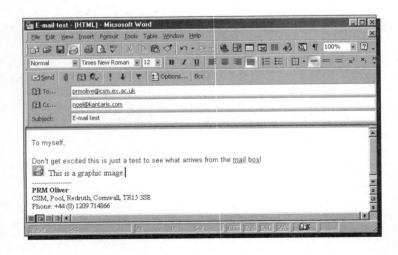

This message was actually sent from one of the authors to himself. A useful exercise when setting up a new e-mail facility, to test it without bothering anybody else! It also shows that you can include graphics in the message, and uses a 'signature' to automatically identify the sender.

When your message is to your complete satisfaction, you just click the **Send** button to send it to the Outlook Outbox. As before, when it is transmitted will depend on your settings in Outlook, but to send all the messages in the Outbox and download any new incoming mail from your server mail box, you can always click the **Send/Receive** button on the Outlook toolbar. The message box below tracks the progress of the sending operation.

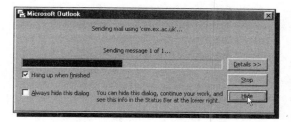

In our case all was well and the message 'bounced' back almost immediately into the Outlook Inbox, as shown below.

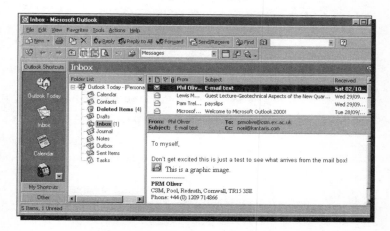

The E-mail Header Buttons

The buttons in the e-mail header control the settings of your messages and have the following functions:

Send	Send the e-mail message to the Outlook Outbox and close the Word window .
	Insert a file as an e-mail attachment.
	Opens the Address Book to select names, or to save the details of new contacts.
	Checks names in the To, Cc and Bcc boxes against those in the address book.
!	Importance: High - Marks the message as being very important.
↓	Importance: Low - Marks the message as not being particularly important.
	Flags a message with a request to the recipient, or a reminder for yourself.
Options...	Opens a dialogue box for you to select from the available message options.
Bcc	Adds a Bcc box to the header if you want to send a 'blind copy' of the message, without the main recipient knowing.
To...	Click to open the Address Book and select a recipient for the message.
Cc...	Click to open the Address Book and select who should receive copies of the message.
Subject:	Type a title for the e-mail message which will appear as a message header.

Using Signatures

An e-mail signature consists of text that is automatically placed at the end of your messages. This usually consists of your name, address, phone number and your Web home page, but some people add lots more.

Word lets you create signatures but the facility is hidden away a little. You use the **Tools**, **Options** menu command, click the **General** tab, click the **E-mail Options** button, and then the **E-mail Signature** tab to finally open the E-mail Options dialogue box shown below.

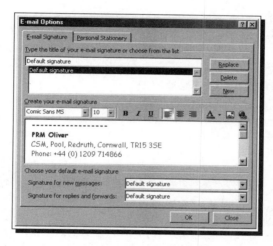

To create a signature, click the **New** button and type a name for it in the top text box. Then click in the **Create your e-mail signature** text box and do just that. The small toolbar above the editing area gives you plenty of control over the font and formatting of the signature text, and even has buttons for adding pictures and hyperlinks. You would use the Insert Hyperlink icon, shown here, to point people towards your own Web site.

You can create different signatures for different types of messages. To make Word use one, by default, select it from the list in the **Signature for new messages** box.

Another method of placing your signatures might be using the AutoText toolbar. To open this bar, right-click on the Word toolbar and select it from the list of different toolbar options. Then when you have completed your message, place the cursor at the
end, click the All
Entries button and
select which signature
you want to use from
the drop-down list, as
shown here. Once you
have placed a

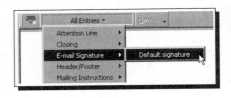

signature on a message, you can right-click in it and choose another (if you have created more) from the list menu that is opened. This is quite a powerful feature.

Personalised Stationery

While the E-mail Options dialogue box is open it is well worth clicking the **Personal Stationery** tab, to open the box shown below, which lets you set what fonts and properties will be used for any new messages you send.

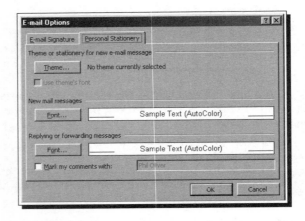

Clicking the **Theme** button opens the box shown on the next page which offers some really spectacular e-mail formatting and background effects.

When you want to send a very special message, maybe like ours above at Christmas, you should be able to find a theme from the **Choose a Theme list**. We will leave it to you to experiment here.

Attaching a File

If you want to send a spreadsheet, Web page, or other type of file as an attachment to your main e-mail message you simply click the **Insert file** Toolbar button and select the file to attach. This opens the Insert File dialogue box, for you to select the file, or files, you want to go with your message.

The attached files are listed in the **Attach** box which opens in the e-mail header section, as shown here. When you send files to others you should make sure that they have a method of accessing the material in the file.

The Address Book

Word has access to quite a useful address book which can make your e-mail life a little easier. To open it you click the Address Book button, shown here, or click on either the **To** or **Cc** buttons. All of these methods open the Select Names dialogue box below.

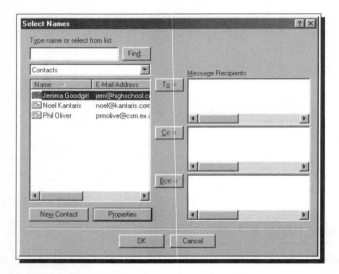

In this box you highlight a contact name in the left window, and click **To** if the main message is being sent to that contact, **Cc** if a copy is being sent to them, or **Bcc** for a blind copy. When the **OK** button is clicked the recipients' e-mail addresses are placed in the message header for you.

Like any address book though, it is only useful if kept up to date! To add a very comprehensive set of details of new friends or business contacts you click the **New Contact** button. You can really go to town here, but don't forget the Data Protection Act!

That should be enough to get you going with Word 2000 as your e-mail editor. Very soon you should find that it becomes just an extension of your usual word processing.

Using Hypertext Links

Hypertext links are elements in a document or Web page that you can click with your mouse, to 'jump to' another document. When clicked they actually fetch another file, or part of a file, to your screen, and the link is the address that uniquely identifies the location of the target file, whether it is located on your PC, on an Intranet, or on the Internet itself. This address is known as a Uniform Resource Locator (URL for short). For a link to an Internet file to work you must obviously have access to the Internet from your PC.

Inserting a Hyperlink

If you know the URL address of the link destination, you can simply type it in a Word document and it will be automatically 'formatted' as a hyperlink by Word. This usually means it will change to bright blue underlined text. In Word a hyperlink consists of the text that the user sees that describes the link, (or an image), the URL of the link's target, and a ScreenTip that appears whenever the 'hand' pointer passes over the link on the screen.

To insert a hyperlink into Word, select the display text or image, and either use the **Insert, Hyperlink** command (<Ctrl+K>), or click the Insert Hyperlink button on the Standard Toolbar. Either action opens a dialogue box, shown below, which allows you to browse for the destination address.

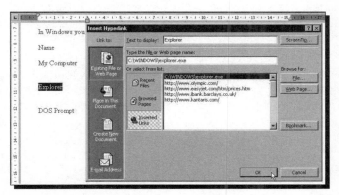

To illustrate the procedure, start Word, open the **PC Users4** memo, and highlight the word 'Explorer' to be found towards the end of it. Next, click the Hyperlink icon and locate the **explorer.exe** file (in the **Windows** folder) using the **Browse** button.

Pressing the **OK** button, underlines the highlighted text and changes its colour to blue. Pointing to such a hyperlink, changes the mouse pointer to a hand, as shown here, and left-clicking it, starts the Explorer. When you have finished using the Explorer, click its Close button for the program to return you automatically to the hyperlinked Word document.

If the location of the file you wanted to hyperlink to is incorrect, or you did not highlight the word to be used as the hyperlink, then errors will occur. If that is the case, place the insertion pointer within the hyperlink word, click the Insert Hyperlink icon again, and press the **Remove Link** button at the bottom left of the displayed Edit Hyperlink dialogue box.

Inserting an Internet Hyperlink

To insert an Internet hyperlink into Word, select the display text or image, and click the Insert Hyperlink button to open the Insert Hyperlink dialogue box below.

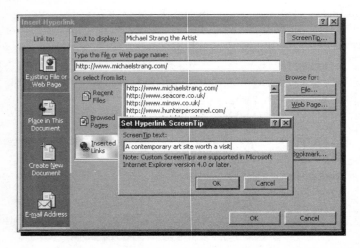

To place an Internet hyperlink, click **Existing File or Web Page** on the 'Link to' bar and enter the hyperlink text in the **Text to display** box. Specify the linked document by either: typing its filename or URL in the **Type the file or Web page name** box, or choosing from the **Or select from list** box. With the latter you have the choice of **Recent Files**, **Browsed Pages**, or **Inserted Links**.

Next, click **Screen Tip** to create a Screen Tip that will be displayed whenever the mouse pointer moves over the hyperlink. Clicking **OK** twite will place the link onto your document. Our example on the last page placed the link shown here. Clicking this link

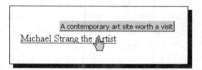

opened our Web browser, loaded the linked Web site into it, and reduced the Word window to an icon on the Start bar.

Inserting Other Hyperlinks

There are three other types of hyperlinks you can place from the Insert Hyperlink box, shown by the other buttons on the **Link to** bar.

To link to a location in the same Word file, click the **Place in This Document** button. Before doing this, though, you should place a bookmark at the link location with the **Insert**, **Bookmark** command, so that you have somewhere to 'jump to'.

To link to a document not yet created, click the **Create New Document** button and enter the name for the new Word file. You can then edit the new file straight away or later on.

If you create a link to an **E-mail Address**, Word will create a new e-mail message with the address already placed in the **To** line of the message header, when the hyperlink is clicked. This type of link is usually used when you want to make it easy for people to contact you.

Drag-and-drop Hyperlinks

You can also create a hyperlink by dragging selected text or a graphic from another Word document, a PowerPoint slide, a range in Excel, or a selected Access database object to your Word document.

To do this, open both files so that they are on the screen at the same time and select the text, graphic, or other item you want to jump to in the destination document. Use the right mouse button to drag the selection to your document, release the mouse button and select **Create Hyperlink Here** from the shortcut menu, as shown here.

Editing Hyperlinks

Once a hyperlink has been placed in a Word document it is very easy to change by right-clicking on it and selecting **Hyperlink** from the drop-down menu. This opens the shortcut menu shown here.

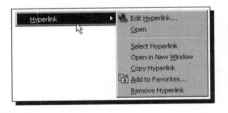

The **Edit Hyperlink** option opens a similar dialogue box to that used for inserting the link in the first place.

You can make any changes you like in this box. The other options on this menu are self explanatory, perhaps the most useful being **Open in New Window** which places the linked information in a new Word window, so you don't 'lose' the current document when the link is activated.

10

Internet Web Pages

The World Wide Web, WWW, or Web as we shall call it, has been responsible for the rapidly expanding popularity of the Internet. When you see the Internet being accessed on TV, what you actually see is a Web page being read on a PC. A Web site is made up of a group of Web pages, all stored on an Internet server. The Web consisting of many millions of such sites, located on server computers around the globe, all of which you can access with the browser software on your own PC. So the Web consists of client computers (yours and mine) and server computers handling multimedia documents with hypertext links built into them (Web pages). Client computers use browser software (such as Navigator and Explorer) to view pages of these documents, one at a time. Server computers use Web server software to maintain the documents for us to access.

With the introduction of Word 2000, Microsoft has gone one step nearer making it possible for anyone to very easily prepare their own Web pages and keep them up to date on their own Internet Web site. This has been done largely with the introduction of Web Folders which, once set up, form shortcuts to the Web servers where Internet Web files are stored. This is a very new concept, and unfortunately at the time of writing, our own ISPs had no facilities to support Web Folders. You may have the same problem, if so we are sure it will only be temporary.

We do not have the space here to fully cover web site design and management, we can only introduce some of Word's useful features. If you want more detail on Web sites generally, may we suggest you read our book *Your own Web site on the Internet*, also published by Bernard Babani (publishing) Ltd.

Creating Web Pages

You can use Word 2000 to create a Web page in the same way you create a 'regular' Word document, by simply saving it as an HTML file, but Word also offers other easy ways to begin Web pages.

Using an Existing Word Document

If you are happy using Word, you can use it to do all your Web editing. The example below is an opening page for a Web site prepared as a normal .doc file in Word.

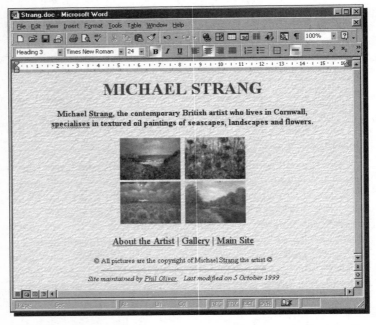

Note that it is shown in Web Layout View, controlled by the buttons on the bottom scroll bar. With this view, Word attempts to show the document as it will appear on the Web. To get an even better idea, you can also use the **File**, **Web Page Preview** command to see the file opened in Internet Explorer, or your default Web browser.

You save an existing, or newly created, document as a Web page with the **File**, **Save as Web Page** menu command. If you want to save the document in a different folder, locate and open the folder and in the **File name** box, type a name for the Web page. While the Save As box is open, as shown below, click the **Change Title** button and type the title you want to appear in the titlebar of the browser when the page is viewed. Click **OK** and then the **Save** button to complete the saving process.

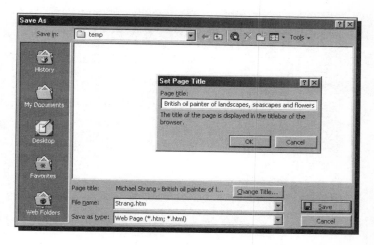

When you save a document as a Web page, all its graphics and objects, such as pictures, AutoShapes, WordArt, text boxes, Equation Editor objects, Organization Chart objects, and Graph objects, are saved as .gif, .jpg, or .png files, so that they can be viewed in a Web browser. When you later reopen the Web page in Microsoft Word, the graphics and objects you see are in their original formats so that you can edit them as normal. Very clever stuff this!

Using the Web Page Wizard

By using the Web Page Wizard, you can create a single Web page or an entire Web site. You can add existing Web pages to your Web site, add a theme and even use frames to improve the look of your Web pages.

Web Page
Wizard

To open the wizard, use the **File**, **New** menu command, click the **Web Pages** tab and double-click the Web Page Wizard icon shown here.

The opening screen of this wizard is shown below. You really must spend a few minutes exploring this feature, it is the best method we have seen so far for easily building Web sites. Amazingly it even lets you use frames, which can be quite tricky to get right.

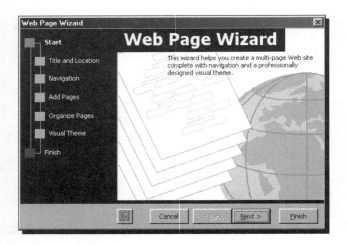

Once you click the **Finish** button to close the wizard, the opening page of your new Web site is opened as a Word document for you to edit and customise to your heart's content.

Using a Web Page Template

When you use a Web page template, Word can make features that are not supported by your target browser unavailable so that you can design impressive Web pages without having to worry about how your formatting will look in a Web browser. You can change your target browser or turn the browser setting off, add a theme and use frames to make your Web pages more dynamic.

The **File**, **New** menu command opens the **New** dialogue box shown below with the Web Pages tab selected.

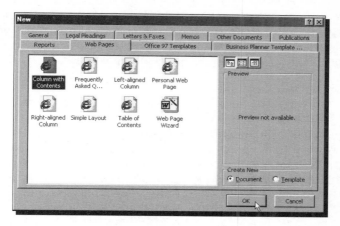

This shows the seven Web page templates that were available to us. Double-clicking a template icon opens an HTML Word document, as shown below. You then have to customise this page with your own contents. Have fun.

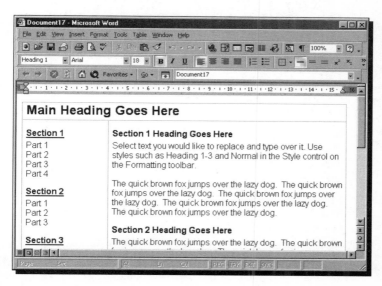

To turn features on or off that are not supported by some Web browsers use the **Tools**, **Options**, menu command, click the **General** tab, followed by **Web Options**, and then click the **General** tab. We suggest you select the **Disable features not supported by** check box and in the **Browser** box, choose 'Microsoft Internet Explorer 4.0 and Netscape Navigator 4.0'. Your pages should then work with most Web browsers used.

Adding a Theme to a Page

As well as the wizard and templates, Word 2000 has a collection of Web page themes that give you a variety of standard page designs, which control the page background, fonts, and colours used in the Web page. You can actually select a theme in the Web Page Wizard, but you can also select one from your Word document. To see some of the effects though, you will have to be in Web Page view. To select a theme, use the **Format**, **Theme** menu command, which opens the following dialogue box.

As you work your way down the list of themes, a sample of each is displayed in the right-hand window pane. The **Style Gallery** option is not of much use for Web pages, but if you find a theme you like you can click the **Set Default** button to have it used for all your new Web pages.

The **Vivid Colors** option makes some of the theme colours even more garish, **Active Graphics** lets you turn on, or off, any moving graphics in the theme, and **Background Image** controls whether you have a theme image or a plain colour as the page background.

Adding Movies and Sounds

With Word 2000 it is easy to add special effects to your Web pages, such as movies or sounds. We don't really recommend it, but you can add an in-line movie, which will be downloaded and played when the page is opened. If you don't want the movie to play whenever the page is opened, you can insert a hyperlink to the movie file, which will then only be downloaded and played when the link is clicked.

To add a background movie, or sound, open the Web

Tools toolbar, shown here, click the Movie, or Sound, button and enter the path or Web address of the movie or sound file you want, or click **Browse** to locate the file.

For a sound file, enter the number of times you want the background sound to repeat, in the **Loop** box.

To be able to hear background sound, a user must have a sound card installed on their computer and their Web browser must support the sound format of the file used. The types of sound files that can be used this way include, .wav, .mid, .au, .aif, .rmi, .snd, and .mp2 (MPEG audio) formats.

The last icon in the Web Tools bar lets you place scrolling text on your page. This can sometimes be useful, but more often is just a distraction! The other Web Tools buttons are to help you build Web page forms.

Some HTML Differences

As we have seen, Word 2000 automatically converts Word's .doc file format to HTML when creating e-mails and Web pages, and back to .doc format when the files are loaded into the word processor. This conversion process is fairly accurate, but by no means perfect because of the basic restrictions inherent in HTML.

With HTML you cannot embed fonts and you have to use tables to control the layout of complex pages. Without them HTML will not let you simulate multiple column layouts, or very specific spacings of text blocks.

To get an idea of the likely differences of formatting of your pages in a Web browser compared to a Word .doc file we suggest you look for the Help section shown below. You should be able to find this in the 'Troubleshoot viewing Web pages' Help topic. You may need to click a few links though.

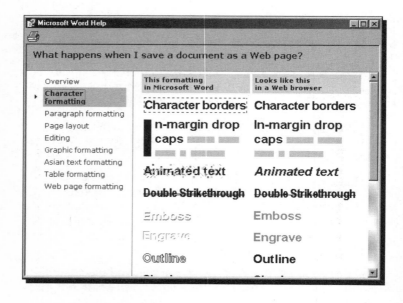

Saving Web Pages on the Internet

If you are lucky and your Web server supports Web Folders, you can use Web folders to save copies of your Web pages to the Web server. Before trying to save and manage folders and files on a Web server, you should contact your system administrator or Internet Service Provider (ISP) to get access and find out the URL, or Web address, you should use.

If your Web server supports File Transfer Protocol (FTP), and most do, you can save or upload your Web pages to an FTP site. Before you try to use FTP, contact your system administrator or ISP to get access details of the location you can save your files to.

Web Folders

A Web folder is a shortcut to a Web server, and lets you very easily publish documents for viewing in Web browsers. To use this feature, the Web server must support Web Folders and unfortunately ours does not. Hopefully, given time, most ISPs will provide this support.

If you find you can use Web folders, you must first add one to your system. In Word 2000, use **File**, **Open**, click the **Web Folders** button and then click the Create New Folder button, as shown below, to start the Add Web Folder Wizard.

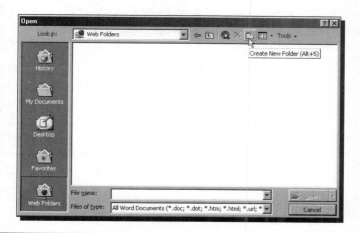

Complete the wizard with the details you obtained from your System Administrator, and as long as you are connected to the Internet a new folder should be placed in your Web Folders section.

Once you have added a Web folder, you can save your Web files and other sub-folders to that location on the Internet server in exactly the same way as you save a file to your hard disc.

Uploading to an FTP Site

Even if your Web server does not support Web folders, it certainly should let you have FTP access to your Web space on the server. Once you have the access details from your System Administrator and before you can save any files to an FTP site, you must add the site to the list of Internet sites on your PC. With Word open, click the Open button on the Standard toolbar, and in the **Look in** box, click **Add/Modify FTP Locations**, to open the dialogue box shown below.

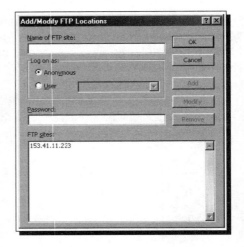

In the **Name of FTP site** box, type the FTP site name given to you by your ISP. This could be a series of numbers separated by dots, or a URL. If you have user privileges for the site, click **User**, and enter your UserID and your password, and click **OK**.

To save a Web page file from Word to your FTP site, and hence make it available over the Internet, first make sure your Internet connection is open. Then use the **File**, **Save As** command and in the **Save in** box, double-click the FTP site you want, as shown here. This should make the

connection to your Web server space, and present you with the list of folders and files that are there. Double-click the location at the site you want, type the document name and click the **Save** button to, hopefully, complete the operation.

In the future, if you need to edit or update a Web page, you can use the Open dialogue box to retrieve the file from your Web server. Once you have carried out your work you can save it back again as described above.

Supporting Files

When you save Web page files from Word 2000 to a Web server or a location on your hard disc, all their supporting files, such as graphics, bullets and background images are, by default, placed in a supporting folder. If you move or copy your Web page to another location, you must also move the supporting folder so that you maintain all links to your Web page.

As an example, if you save a Web page called Page1.htm, its bullets and other graphic files would be stored in a 'supporting files' folder called "Page1_files". So if you move the file Page1.htm, you must also move the supporting files folder (Page1_files) to the new location.

By default, the name of the supporting folder is the name of the Web page plus an underscore (_), a period (.), or a hyphen (-), followed by the word "files".

11

Sharing Information

You can link or embed all or part of an existing file created either in an Office application or in any other application that supports Object Linking and Embedding (OLE). However, if an application does not support OLE, then you must use the copy/cut and paste commands to copy or move information from one application to another. In general, you copy, move, link, embed, or hyperlink information depending on the imposed situation, as follows:

Imposed Situation	*Method to Adopt*
Inserted information will not need updating, or Application does not support OLE.	Copy or move
Inserted information needs to be automatically updated in the destination file as changes are made to the data in the source file, or Source file will always be available and you want to minimise the size of the destination file, or Source file is to be shared amongst several users.	Link
Inserted information might need to be updated but source file might not be always accessible, or Destination files needs to be edited without having these changes reflected in the source file.	Embed
To jump to a location in a document or Web page, or to a file that was created in a different program.	Hyperlink

Copying or Moving Information

To copy or move information between programs running under Windows, such as Microsoft applications, is extremely easy. To move information, use the drag and drop facility, while to copy information, use the **Edit, Copy** and **Edit, Paste** commands.

To illustrate the technique, you will need to either create an Excel file, or have such a file on disc. We will copy into Word our created Excel file **Project.xls**, considering the following two possibilities:

Source File Available without Application

Let us assume that you only have the source file **Project.xls** on disc, but not the application that created it (that is you don't have Excel). In such a situation, you can only copy the contents of the whole file to the destination (in our case Word). To achieve this, do the following:

*   Start Word and minimise it on the Taskbar.

*   Use My Computer (or Explorer) to locate the file whose contents you want to copy into Word.

*   Click the filename that you want to copy, hold the mouse button down and point to Word on the Taskbar until the application opens.

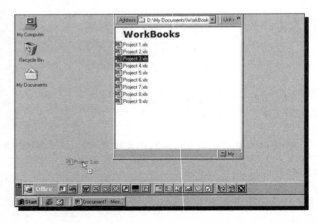

- While still holding the mouse button down, move the mouse pointer into Word's open document to the exact point where you would like to insert the contents of **Project.xls**.

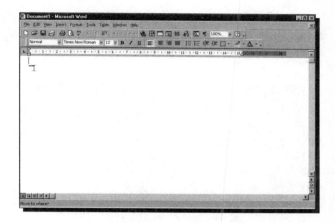

- Release the mouse button to place the contents of **Project.xls** into Word at that point.

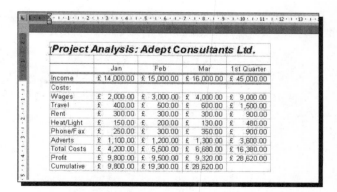

Do remember, however, that only the active sheet of the relevant workbook will be copied with this method.

Source File and Application Available

Assuming that you have both the file and the application that created it on your computer, you can copy all or part of the contents of the source file to the destination file. To achieve this, do the following:

- Start Excel and open **Project.xls**.

- Highlight as much information as you would like to copy and click the copy icon on the Toolbar.

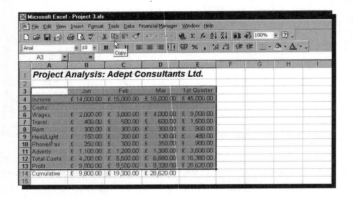

- Start Word and click the Paste icon on the Toolbar.

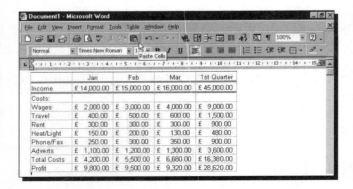

Insert an Excel Worksheet in Word

If the 'Insert Excel Worksheet' button, shown here, appears on your Word Toolbar, you can use it to insert a worksheet of the required number of rows and columns, by simply clicking the button and dragging down to the right. As you drag the mouse, the 'Worksheet' button expands to create the grid of rows and columns, shown below, in a similar manner to that of creating rows and columns of tables.

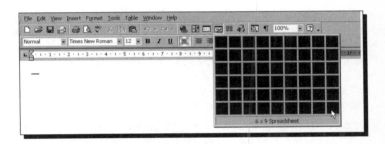

When you release the mouse button, the worksheet is inserted in your Word document. You can then insert data and apply functions to them. To see which functions are available, use the **Insert, Function** command.

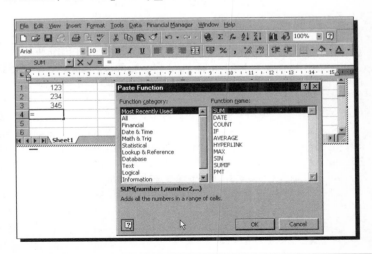

Object Linking and Embedding

Object Linking is copying information from one file (the source file) to another file (the destination file) and maintaining a connection between the two files. When information in the source file is changed, then the information in the destination file is automatically updated. Linked data is stored in the source file, while the file into which you place the data stores only the location of the source and displays a representation of the linked data.

For example, you would use Object Linking if you would want an Excel chart included in, say, a Word document to be updated whenever you changed the information used to create the chart in the first place within Excel. In such a case, the Excel worksheet containing the chart would be referred to as the source file, while the Word document would be referred to as the destination file.

Object Embedding is inserting information created in one file (the source file) into another file (the container file). After such information has been embedded, the object becomes part of the container file. When you double-click an embedded object, it opens in the application in which it was created in the first place. You can then edit it in place, and the original object in the source application remains unchanged.

Thus, the main differences between linking and embedding are where the data is stored and how it is updated after you place it in your file. Linking saves you disc space as only one copy of the linked object is kept on disc. Embedding a logo chosen for your headed paper, saves the logo with every saved letter!

In what follows, we will discuss how you can link or embed either an entire file or selected information from an existing file, and how you can edit an embedded object. Furthermore, we will examine how to mail merge a letter written in Word with a list created either in Access, Excel, Outlook, or even Word itself.

Embedding a New Object

To embed a new object into an application, do the following:

- Open the container file, say Word, and click where you want to embed the new object.

- Use the **Insert, Picture** command, to display the additional drop-down menu, shown below.

- From this last drop-down menu action **Clip Art**, click the category you want and select a graphic.

As an example, we selected **Clip Art** (you could select a different option) and chose the Animal category from which we selected the graphic shown here. Clicking the **Insert Clip** button on the drop-down menu, embeds the selected object within Word.

Right-clicking such an embedded object displays a drop-down menu and selecting the **Edit Picture** option, opens up the Draw application which we used to add the perch. Once an embedded picture has been edited, double-clicking on it opens up the application used to edit it in the first place (the Draw application in our case), otherwise it opens the Format Picture dialogue box. Do try it for yourself.

Linking or Embedding an Existing File

To embed an existing file in its entirety into another application, do the following:

- Open the container file, say Word, and click where you want to embed the file.

- Use the **Insert, Object** command, to open the Object dialogue box, shown below, when the **Create from File** tab is clicked.

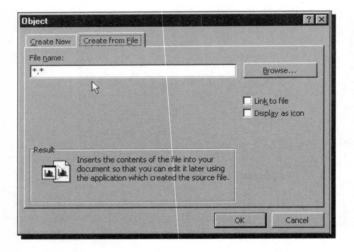

To locate the file you want to link or embed, click **Browse**, and then select the options you want.

- In the **File Name** box, type the name of the file you want to link or embed.

- To maintain a link to the original file, check the **Link to file** box.

Note: To insert graphics files, use the **Insert, Picture, From File** command instead of the **Insert, Object** command. This displays the Insert Picture dialogue box which allows you to specify within the **Look in** box the folder and file you want to insert.

Linking or Embedding Selected Information

To link or embed selected information from an existing file created in one application into another, do the following:

- Select the information in the source file you want to link or embed.

- Use the **Edit, Copy** command to copy the selected information to the Clipboard.

- Switch to the container file or document in which you want to place the information, and then click where you want the information to appear.

- Use the **Edit, Paste Special** command to open the following dialogue box:

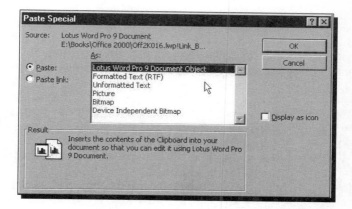

- To link the information, click the **Paste link** radio button, or to embed the information, click the **Paste** radio button. In the **As** box, click the item with the word 'Object' in its name. For example, if you copied the information from a Lotus Word Pro document, as we have for this example, the Word Pro Document Object appears in the **As** box. Select this object and press **OK**.

Editing an Embedded Object

If the application in which you created an embedded object is installed on your computer, double-click the object to open it for editing. Some applications start the original application in a separate window and then open the object for editing, while other applications temporarily replace the menus and toolbars in the current application so that you can edit the embedded object in place, without switching to another window.

If the application in which an embedded object was created is not installed on your computer, convert the object to the file format of an application you do have. For example, if your Word document contains an embedded Microsoft Works Spreadsheet object and you do not have Works, you can convert the object to an Excel Workbook format and edit it in Excel.

Some embedded objects, such as sound and video clips, when double-clicked start playing their contents, instead of opening an application for editing. To illustrate this, copy either the **tutor.mpg** media file from its folder in the Windows 98 CD or the **goodtime.avi** video file from its folder in the Windows 95 CD, into Word using the **Copy, Paste Special** command (click the **Paste** radio button and the **Display as**

icon box on the displayed dialogue box), and click **OK** to paste the required icon. The **tutor** file is to be found in the **cdsample, videos** folder, while the **goodtime** file is to be found in the **funstaff, videos, highperf** folder. The

former places a Windows Media Player icon in your document, as shown here. Double-clicking such an icon, starts the video.

To edit one of these objects, select it and use the **Edit {Media Clip Object}, Edit** command. What appears within the curly brackets here, depends on the selected object; media clip in this case. Of course, unless you have the facilities required for editing such objects, you will be unable to do so.

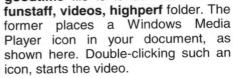

Mail Merging Lists

There are times when you may want to send the same basic letter to several different people, or companies. The easiest way to do this is with a Merge operation. Two files are prepared; a 'Data' file with the names and addresses, and a 'Form' file, containing the text and format of the letter. The two files are then merged together to produce a third file containing an individual letter to each party listed in the original data file.

Before creating a list of names and addresses for a mail merge, you need to select the Office application that is most suited to the task. For a mail merge, you can use a list you create in Access, Excel, Outlook, or Microsoft Word.

- For a long list in which you expect to add, change, or delete records, and for which you want powerful sorting and searching capabilities at your disposal, you should use either Access or Excel, then specify the appropriate data file in the Word Mail Merge Helper (see below).

- To use the list of names and addresses in your Outlook Contact List, you select this list in the Word Mail Merge Helper.

- For a small to medium size list of names and addresses in which you do not expect to make many changes, you could elect to create a list in the Word Mail Merge Helper.

The Word Mail Merger Helper is a dialogue box in which you specify:

(a) whether you want to create form letters, labels, or print envelopes,

(b) where your list of names and addresses (data) is to be found, and

(c) what query options are to be applied to your data list before the merging process starts. These will be explained next with illustrated examples.

We will illustrate the merge procedure by using a memo created in Word (**PC Users1**) and a table which can be created in Word, or already exists either in an electronic book such as Outlook, in Excel or in an Access table.

No matter which method you choose, first start Word and open the **PC Users1** memo (or your own letter), then provide two empty lines at the very top of the memo/letter by placing the insertion pointer at the beginning of the memo and pressing <Enter> twice. Then select these two empty lines and choose the Normal paragraph style.

Next, select **Tools, Mail Merge** which displays the Mail Merge Helper dialogue box shown below.

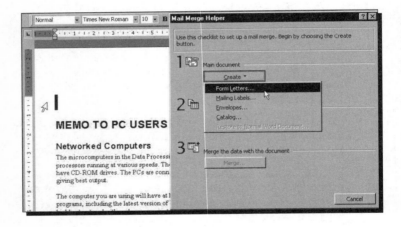

In this box, you define in three successive steps:

1. The document to be used,
2. The source of your data, and
3. The merging of the two.

Start by clicking the **Create** button, select the **Form Letters** option, and click the **Active Window** button.

Next, click the **Get Data** button which causes a drop-down menu to display, shown below.

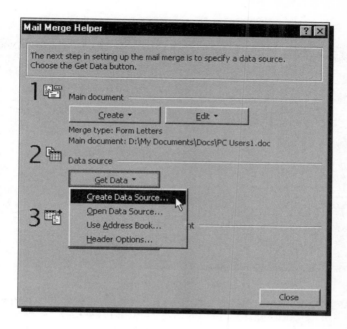

It is from this menu that you can select either to create your data source (the list of addresses) in Word, open (or import) an existing list of addresses which might be found in either Word, Excel, Access, etc., or use a list of contacts in an electronic address book such as Outlook.

In what follows, we will examine each of these options (in the same order as the list in the above drop-down menu). You can, of course, skip the Create an Address List in Word section, if you already have an existing data list.

Creating an Address List in Word

Selecting the **Create Data Source** menu option, displays the following dialogue box.

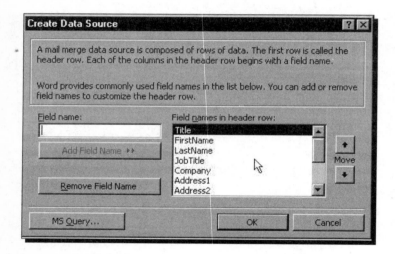

As you can see, Word provides commonly used field names for your address list. Unwanted field names can be deleted from the list by selecting them and pressing the **Remove Field Name** button. To add your own field name, type it in the **Field Name** box and press the **Add Field Name** button. The **Move** buttons to the right of the list can be used to move a selected field in the list to the top or bottom of the list by pressing the up-arrow or down-arrow, respectively.

Having compiled the required field names for your list, pressing the **OK** button displays a Save As dialogue box, in which you can name your data list, say **Address**. Word automatically adds the file extension **.doc**, and displays the following warning dialogue box which allows you to either edit the data source or the main document.

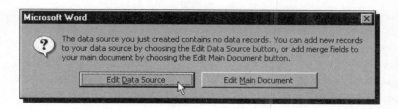

Press the **Edit Data Source** button if you want to create or edit your data list. Doing so displays the following Data Form dialogue box.

Here you can create a new data list or edit an existing one. We have typed in one fictitious entry in order to demonstrate the process, but we have not attempted to change the field names provided in any way whatsoever.

Having created a Word data list, added to one or edited one, pressing **OK** saves your changes to the already existing filename.

What follows is common to all existing data files, no matter in which application you chose to create them.

Getting an Address List

If you have not done so already, open the letter you want to mail merge, place the cursor in the position you want the address to appear, and select **Tools, Mail Merge** in Word. Then press the **Create** button in the Mail Merge Helper and choose **Form Letters**, **Active Window**.

Next, click the **Get Data** button (the 2nd step in the Mail Merge Helper) which causes a drop-down menu, shown here, to display.

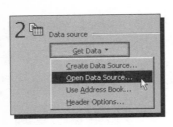

Select the **Open Data Source** option, and in the displayed dialogue box, select the drive, and click the down-arrow on the **Files of type** box. From here you can choose the type of file that holds your address list, which could be one created in Word or a text editor (or exported in that form from another application), or an Access or Excel file.

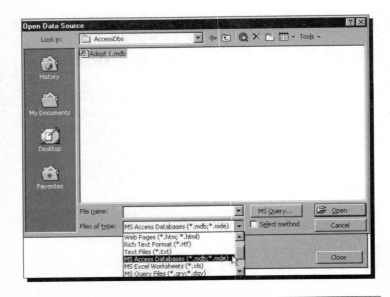

For our example we chose the **MS Access Database** type of file, which lists the databases on the specified drive and path. Next, select the database that holds your address data and click the **Open** button. Access is then loaded and the tables within the selected database are listed. Choose the Table that contains your data and click the **OK** button.

Microsoft Word now displays a warning message, shown below, to the effect that no merge fields have been found in your document.

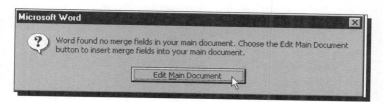

Don't worry about this, as we will rectify this omission, as follows:

- Click the **Edit Main Document** button on the above warning box which displays your document with an additional toolbar below the Formatting bar, as follows:

- Click the **Insert Merge Field** button on the new toolbar. This displays the fields in your Customers table.

- Select in turn, Name, Address, Town, County, and Post_Code. The first three are placed on the document on separate lines (by pressing <Enter> after each selection), while the last two are placed on the same line, but separated by a space. Finally, type on a new line the letters FAO: plus a space, and place the Contact field against it.

The first few lines of your document should now look as follows (we have typed in the word FAO: on the last line of the address, before inserting the 'Contact' field.

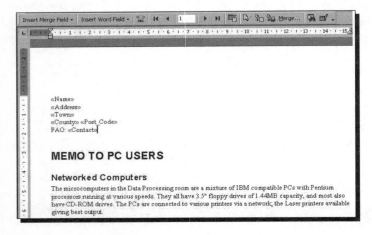

- Click the View Merged Data icon, shown to the right, to see your merged data. Clicking this icon once more, returns you to the screen above so that you can edit your work, or add merge fields.

- Click either the Merge to New Document icon or the Merge to Printer icon to create a new merged document to file or send the merged document to the printer.

That's all there is to it. You will possibly find it takes as little time to do, as it did to read about it!

12

Customising Word 2000

Word Macro Basics

A macro is simply a set of instructions made up of a sequence of keystrokes, mouse selections, or commands stored in a macro file. After saving, or writing, a macro and attaching a quick key combination to it, you can run the same sequence of commands whenever you want. This can save a lot of time and, especially with repetitive operations, can save mistakes creeping into your work.

In Word there are two basic ways of creating macros. The first one is generated by the program itself, recording and saving a series of keystrokes, or mouse clicks. The second one involves the use of Word Visual Basic, the programming language that is common to all Office 2000 applications. With this method, you can write quite complex macro programs directly into a macro file using the Visual Basic editor.

Recording a Macro

To demonstrate how easy it is to save and name a macro, we will start with a simplistic one that enhances the word at the cursor to bold type in italics. Open **PC Users1**, place the cursor in a document word and either double-click the **REC** button on the Status bar, shown below, or select the **Tools, Macro, Record New Macro** command.

Either of these, opens the Record Macro dialogue box shown below. In the **Macro name** input box, type a name for your macro (call it BoldItalic), then give your macro a **Description** (such as Bold & Italic) and click on the **Keyboard** button.

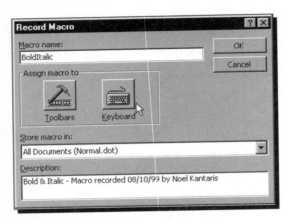

In the displayed Customize dialogue box, press a suitable key stroke combination, such as <Ctrl+Shift+I>, in the **Press new shortcut key** input box.

The shortcut key combination will appear in the input box and immediately below it you will be informed whether this key combination is currently attached to an internal macro or not, as shown below.

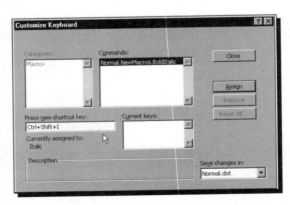

Most <Ctrl>, or <Shift> keys with a letter or function key combinations are suitable (the word [unassigned] will appear under the **Currently assigned to:** heading) if the chosen combination of keys is not already assigned to a macro. Our choice of key strokes results in the message 'Italic', under the **Currently assigned to:** heading. This does not matter in this instance, because both the key combinations <Ctrl+I> and <Ctrl+Shift+I> are assigned to Italic, so we can use one. To clear an entry in this text box, press the <BkSp> key.

Next, press the **Assign** button followed by the **Close** button. From this point on, all key strokes and mouse clicks (but not mouse movements in the editing area) will be recorded. To indicate that the recorder is on, Word attaches a recorder graphic to the mouse pointer, as shown here. Word also displays the Stop and Pause buttons to allow you to stop or pause a macro.

A macro can also be stopped by double-clicking at the REC button on the Status bar.

While the cursor is still placed in the word to be modified, use the key strokes, <Ctrl+→> to move to the end of the current word followed by <Shift+Ctrl+←> to highlight it, click the Bold and Italic buttons on the Formatting toolbar, press <→> to cancel the highlight and click the Stop button on the Macro Record toolbar. Your macro should now be recorded and held in memory.

Saving a Macro to Disc

To save your macro to disc, use the **File, Save As** command and give your macro the name **Macro 1** and in the **Save as type** box select 'Document Template (*.dot)'. If you quit Word without saving the template, you will be asked if you want to save the changes made to the template. Choose the **Yes** button to save your macro.

Please note: If your PC is Virus protected, particularly by a program that stops macros writing to your hard disc, you must disable it first before you can save this macro.

Playing Back a Macro

There are four main ways of running a macro. You can use the playback shortcut keys straight from the keyboard; in our case place the cursor in another word and press <Ctrl+Shift+I>. The word should be enhanced automatically. If not, check back that you carried out the instructions correctly.

The second method is to select the **Tools**, **Macro, Macros** command, then select the macro from the list, as shown below, and press the **Run** button.

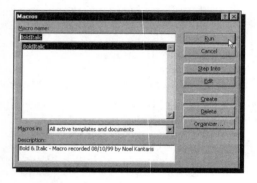

From this dialogue box you can also **Edit**, **Delete**, or select the **Organizer** to display a similarly named dialogue box, shown below, so that you can, amongst other housekeeping facilities, **Rename** your macro.

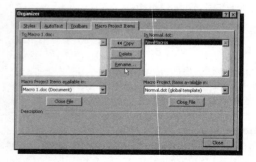

Attaching Macros/Commands to a Toolbar

The last two methods of activating a macro are to attach it to a custom button on a toolbar or a menu, and simply click the button or the menu option.

To assign a macro to a toolbar, use the **Tools, Customize** command, click the **Commands** tab and select **Macros** from the **Categories** list of the displayed dialogue box, shown below.

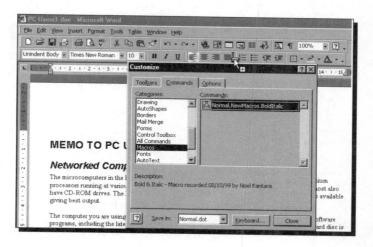

Next, click the macro from the **Commands** list to see its description and drag the macro name to any button on one of the toolbars. The selected macro inserts its *name* before the button pointed to on the toolbar.

To assign this macro to a button on the toolbar, click the **Modify Selection** button on the Customize dialogue box, select the **Change Button Image** option from the displayed menu list and choose a button from the palette shown on your screen (we chose the smiling face), as shown overleaf. Finally, you can select to display on the toolbar either the button only by clicking the **Text Only (in Menus)** or **Default Style** option, or both the button and its description by clicking the **Image and Text** option.

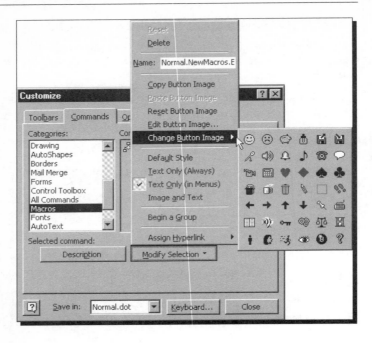

In general, you can create toolbar buttons for commands and frequently used styles, AutoText entries, and fonts. For more detail on this subject, look up the 'Add or Remove Toolbar Buttons' section further on in this chapter.

Removing Macro or Command Buttons

To remove a macro or command button from a toolbar, use the **Tools, Customize** command, click the **Commands** tab and drag the button representing your macro or command from its position on the toolbar on to the editing area of your document.

Editing a Macro

You can edit the entries in a macro file by selecting the **Tools**, **Macro**, **Macros**, command which opens the Macro dialogue box, shown below, in which you select the macro file to edit.

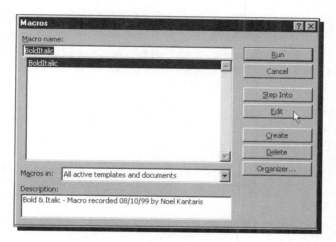

Select the macro you want to edit and press the **Edit** button. Word loads the file into the normal editing screen and you treat the macro file exactly the same as any other. The listing of our **Macro 1** file should look as follows:

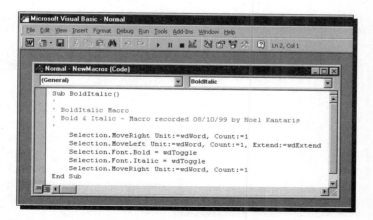

If you look at this listing you will see that it would be very easy to edit the commands in the file. If you do edit it, you should then save the file with the **File, Save Normal** command.

Notice the following two aspects in the screen display above:

(a)   When editing a macro, the Toolbar is replaced by a Visual Basic Standard toolbar, and

(b)   Macros within Visual Basic are considered to be 'subroutines' that run under an Office 2000 application, Word 2000 in this case.

It is easy to make small changes to macros you have recorded using the buttons on the Macro Editing bar. However, if you wanted to create a macro that executed commands which could not be recorded, such as switching to a particular folder and displaying the Open dialogue box, then you must learn to use the Visual Basic programming language.

To return to your document from a Visual Basic screen, click the Word icon at the top-left corner of the toolbar.

Getting Help with Macros

There are far too many aspects to macros that we could not hope to cover in a general book on Word. We, therefore, suggest you activate the Assistant and ask for help on 'macros', as shown below.

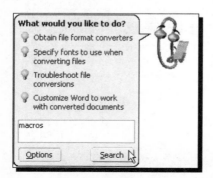

Clicking the **Search** button, displays the help screen shown on the next page. In this composite screen dump, we show both sides of the help screen. Do spend some time looking up each topic in turn. You will learn a lot. Try it!

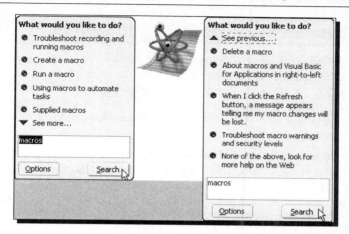

If you have installed the complete Word 2000 package, then you will have access to the Word Visual Basic Help by using the **Help** menu option once the Visual Basic Editor is actioned, as shown below.

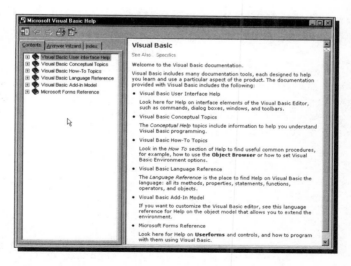

Within the listed help topics, you should find a wealth of information, showing you how to program your macros and how to use the various built-in functions.

Customising Toolbars and Menus

We have already touched on the subject of customising a Word toolbar when we showed you how to place a macro button on one of them. What follows is a more detailed account of how you can customise both toolbars and menus to your specific requirements, including the creation of your own toolbar.

Word 2000, as well as all the other components of Office 2000, provide you with 'intelligent' toolbars and menus that monitor the way you work and make sure that the tools you use most often are available to you on them. However, if you want to use some new tool which is not on a displayed toolbar or menu, you are in trouble - you will have to look for it amongst a wealth of tools which can be activated in a number of different ways! What we will try to do here, is to show you how you could increase your working efficiency, in the shortest possible time.

The Default Toolbars and Menus

A toolbar can contain buttons with images, menus, or a combination of both. Word includes many built-in toolbars that you can show and hide as needed by using the **View, Toolbars** command which opens the cascade menu shown to the left. To activate a toolbar, left-click it, which causes a small check mark to appear against it. By default, the Standard and Formatting built-in toolbars are docked side by side below the menu bar.

You can move toolbars by dragging the move handle on a docked toolbar, shown to the right, or drag the title bar on a floating toolbar to another location. If you drag the toolbar to the edge of the program window or to a location beside another docked toolbar, it becomes a docked toolbar.

As we have seen in earlier chapters, when you first start Word, both active toolbars and short menus display standard buttons and basic commands. As you work with the program, the buttons and commands that you use most often are displayed on the toolbars and short menus. Both toolbars and menus can be expanded to show more buttons and commands by simply clicking the ▪ (**More Buttons**) at the end of the toolbar, or the ⯆ (double-arrow) at the bottom of the short menu.

To show the full set of buttons on a toolbar, drag the toolbar to a location other than the edge of the program window. To see more toolbars than those displayed when using the **View, Toolbars** command, use the **Tools, Customize** command to open the Customize dialogue box shown below, but click the Toolbars tab.

To show the full set of menu commands, click the Options tab of the Customize dialogue box, shown below, then check and/or uncheck options as required.

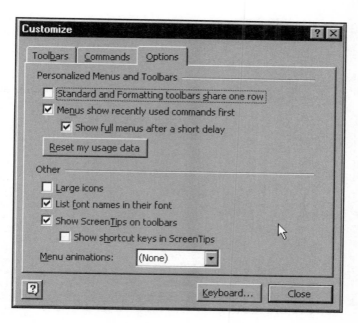

Move or Copy Toolbar Buttons

If you wish to move or copy a toolbar button from one toolbar to another, use the **View, Toolbars** command and check both toolbars, so they are visible on your screen. Then do one of the following:

- To move a toolbar button, hold down the <Alt> key and drag the button to the new location on the same toolbar or onto another toolbar.

- To copy a toolbar button, hold down both the <Ctrl+Alt> keys and drag the button to the new location.

Add or Remove Toolbar Buttons

To add a button to a toolbar, first display the toolbar in question, then use the **Tools, Customize** command to open the Customize dialogue box, shown below, with the Commands tab selected.

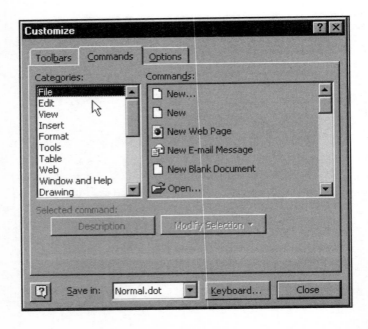

Then do the following:

- In the **Categories** box, click a category for the command you want the button to perform. For example, click Macros to add a button that runs a macro, click Styles to add a button that applies a style, click AutoText to add a button that inserts an AutoText entry, or click Fonts to add a button that applies a particular font.

- Drag the command or macro you want from the **Commands** box to the displayed toolbar.

Note: If you don't see the command you want under a particular category, click All Commands in the **Categories** box.

To quickly add a built-in button to a built-in toolbar, click on ⚇ (**More Buttons**) on a docked toolbar (or click the ◪ (down-arrow) in the upper-left corner of a floating toolbar, then click **Add or Remove Buttons** and select the check box next to the button you want to add.

To remove a button from a displayed toolbar, hold the <Alt> button down and drag the unwanted button from its position on the toolbar on to the editing area of your document. When you remove a built-in toolbar button, the button is still available in the Customize dialogue box. However, when you remove a custom toolbar button, it is permanently deleted. To remove and save a custom toolbar button for later use, you should create a 'storage toolbar' as described below.

Create a Custom Toolbar

To create a custom toolbar, carry out the following steps:

- Display the toolbars that contain the buttons (whether custom or built-in buttons) you want to copy, move, or store in a custom toolbar.

- Use the **Tools**, **Customize** command, and click the Toolbars tab of the displayed dialogue box.

- Click the **New** button to display the screen shown below.

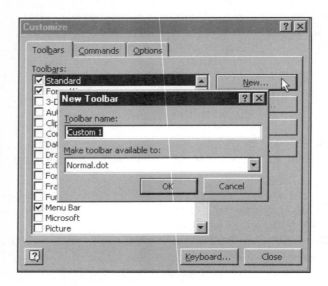

- In the **Toolbar name** text box, type the name you want, and in the **Make toolbar available to** box, click the template or document you want to save the toolbar in, and then click **OK**.

- Finally, click the **Close** button. The new toolbar remains showing on the screen.

You can now use the skills acquired earlier to move and/or copy buttons to the new toolbar. If the newly created toolbar is for 'storing' deleted custom-made buttons, then you might like to hide it by right-clicking it and clearing the check box next to its name in the shortcut menu.

Manipulating Menu Commands

Menu commands can be added to or removed from menus in the same way as buttons can be added to or removed from toolbars. You could even add menus to a button on a toolbar.

For example, to add a command or other item to a menu, do the following:

* Use the **Tools**, **Customize** command to open the Customize dialogue box, then click the Commands tab.

* In the **Categories** box, click a category for the command.

* Drag the command you want from the **Commands** box over the menu. When the menu displays a list of menu options, point to the location where you want the command to appear on the menu, and then release the mouse, as shown below.

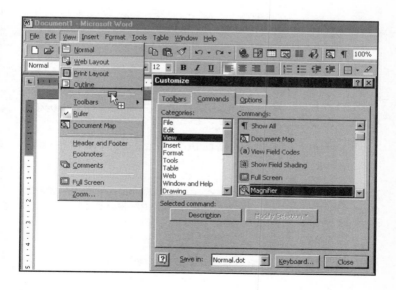

If you don't see the command you want under a particular category, click All Commands in the Categories box.

To remove a command from a list of menu options, do the following:

- Open the Customize dialogue box (you might have to move it out of the way of the drop-down menu options from which you want to remove a command).

- Select the menu option you want to remove and drag it to the editing area of your document, as shown below.

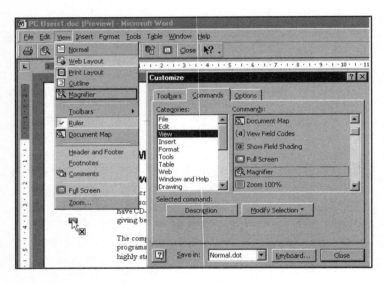

- Release the mouse button to delete the unwanted menu option.

As you can see, manipulating menu options is very similar to manipulating buttons on toolbars, so we leave it to you to explore all the available possibilities - have fun!

Restoring Default Toolbars or Menus

To restore the default buttons on toolbars or menu options, use the **Tools**, **Customize** command to open the Customize dialogue box. Leave the Customize box open (you might need to move it out of the way), and do one of the following:

For a toolbar:

- Use the **Tools, Customize** command, and then click the Toolbars tab.

- In the **Toolbars** box, click the name of the toolbar you want to reset original buttons and menus on.

- Click the **Reset** button to open the Reset Toolbar dialogue box.

- In the Reset changes text box, click the template or document that contains the changes you want to reset.

For a menu:

- Use the **Tools, Customize** command, and then click the Commands tab.

- Click the menu that contains the command you want to restore. Right-click the menu command, and then click **Reset** on the shortcut menu.

Getting Help on Toolbars and Menus

Word 2000 has a wealth of help screens on toolbars and menus. To look at some of these, simply activate the Office Assistant, and search for 'menus'. The Assistant returns the list of topics shown below.

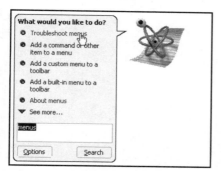

We suggest you spend some time looking at the various help topics. For example, clicking the first entry under 'What would you like to do?', opens the Microsoft Word Help screen shown on the next page.

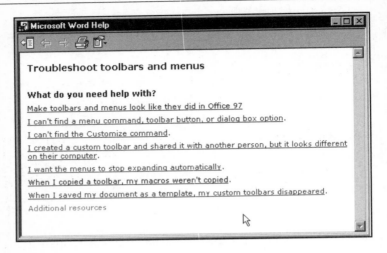

That is about it. We hope you have enjoyed reading this book as much as we have enjoyed writing it. Of course Word 2000 is capable of a lot more than we have discussed here, but what we have tried to do is to give you enough information so that you can forge ahead and explore by yourself the rest of its capabilities.

A glossary is included next, for reference, and in case you have trouble with any jargon that may have crept in.

13

Glossary of Terms

ActiveX	A set of technologies that enables software components to interact with one another in a networked environment, regardless of the language in which the components were created.
Add-in	A mini-program which runs in conjunction with another and enhances its functionality.
Address	A unique number or name that identifies a specific computer or user on a network.
Anonymous FTP	Anonymous FTP allows you to connect to a remote computer and transfer public files back to your local computer without the need to have a user ID and password.
Application	Software (program) designed to carry out certain activity, such as word processing, or data management.
Applet	A program that can be downloaded over a network and launched on the user's computer.
Archie	Archie is an Internet service that allows you to locate files that can be downloaded via FTP.

ASP	Active Server Page. File format used for dynamic Web pages that get their data from a server based database.
Association	An identification of a filename extension to a program. This lets Windows open the program when its files are selected.
ASCII	A binary code representation of a character set. The name stands for 'American Standard Code for Information Interchange'.
Authoring	The process of creating web documents or software.
AVI	Audio Video Interleaved. A Windows multimedia file format for sound and moving pictures.
Backbone	The main transmission lines of the Internet, running at over 45Mbps.
Backup	To make a back-up copy of a file or a disc for safekeeping.
Bandwidth	The range of transmission frequencies a network can use. The greater the bandwidth the more information that can be transferred over a network.
Banner	An advertising graphic shown on a Web page.
BASIC	Beginner's All-purpose Symbolic Instruction Code - a high-level programming language.
BBS	Bulletin Board System, a computer equipped with software and telecoms links that allow it to act as an information host for remote computer systems.

Beta test	A test of software that is still under development, by people actually using the software.
BinHex	A file conversion format that converts binary files to ASCII text files.
Bitmap	A technique for managing the image displayed on a computer screen.
Bookmark	A marker inserted at a specific point in a document to which the user may wish to return for later reference.
Bound control	A control on a database form, report or data access page that is tied to a field in an underlying table or query.
Browse	A button in some Windows dialogue boxes that lets you view a list of files and folders before you make a selection.
Browser	A program, like the Internet Explorer, that lets you view Web pages.
Bug	An error in coding or logic that causes a program to malfunction.
Button	A graphic element in a dialogue box or toolbar that performs a specified function.
Cache	An area of memory, or disc space, reserved for data, which speeds up downloading.
Card	A removable printed-circuit board that is plugged into a computer expansion slot.
CD-ROM	Compact Disc - Read Only Memory; an optical disc which information may be read from but not written to.

CGI	Common Gateway Interface - a convention for servers to communicate with local applications and allow users to provide information to scripts attached to web pages, usually through forms.
Cgi-bin	The most common name of a directory on a web server in which CGI programs are stored.
Chart	A graphical view of data that is used to visually display trends, patterns, and comparisons.
Click	To press and release a mouse button once without moving the mouse.
Client	A computer that has access to services over a computer network. The computer providing the services is a server.
Client application	A Windows application that can accept linked, or embedded, objects.
Clipboard	A temporary storage area of memory, where text and graphics are stored with the Windows cut and copy actions.
Command	An instruction given to a computer to carry out a particular action.
Compressed file	One that is compacted to save server space and reduce transfer times. Typical file extensions for compressed files include .zip (DOS/Windows) and .tar (UNIX).
Configuration	A general purpose term referring to the way you have your computer set up.

Controls	Objects on a form, report, or data access page that display data, perform actions, or are used for decoration.
Cookies	Files stored on your hard drive by your Web browser that hold information for it to use.
CPU	The Central Processing Unit; the main chip that executes all instructions entered into a computer.
Cyberspace	Originated by William Gibson in his novel 'Neuromancer', now used to describe the Internet and the other computer networks.
Data access page	A Web page, created by Access, that has a connection to a database; you can view, add, edit, and manipulate the data in this page.
Database	A collection of data related to a particular topic or purpose.
DBMS	Database management system - A software interface between the database and the user.
Dial-up Connection	A popular form of Net connection for the home user, over standard telephone lines.
Direct Connection	A permanent connection between your computer system and the Internet.
Default	The command, device or option automatically chosen.
Desktop	The Windows screen working background, on which you place icons, folders, etc.

Device driver	A special file that must be loaded into memory for Windows to be able to address a specific procedure or hardware device.
Device name	A logical name used by DOS to identify a device, such as LPT1 or COM1 for the parallel or serial printer.
Dialogue box	A window displayed on the screen to allow the user to enter information.
Directory	An area on disc where information relating to a group of files is kept. Also known as a folder.
Disc	A device on which you can store programs and data.
Disconnect	To detach a drive, port or computer from a shared device, or to break an Internet connection.
Document	A file produced by an application program. When used in reference to the Web, a document is any file containing text, media or hyperlinks that can be transferred from an HTTP server to a browser.
Domain	A group of devices, servers and computers on a network.
Domain Name	The name of an Internet site, for example www.michaelstrang.com, which allows you to reference Internet sites without knowing their true numerical address.
DOS	Disc Operating System. A collection of small specialised programs that allow interaction between user and computer.

Double-click	To quickly press and release a mouse button twice.
Download	To transfer to your computer a file, or data, from another computer.
DPI	Dots Per Inch - a resolution standard for laser printers.
Drag	To move an object on the screen by pressing and holding down the left mouse button while moving the mouse.
Drive name	The letter followed by a colon which identifies a floppy or hard disc drive.
EISA	Extended Industry Standard Architecture, for construction of PCs with the Intel 32-bit micro-processor.
Embedded object	Information in a document that is 'copied' from its source application. Selecting the object opens the creating application from within the document.
Engine	Software used by search services.
E-mail	Electronic Mail - A system that allows computer users to send and receive messages electronically.
Ethernet	A very common method of networking computers in a LAN.
FAQ	Frequently Asked Questions - A common feature on the Internet, FAQs are files of answers to commonly asked questions.
FAT	The File Allocation Table. An area on disc where information is kept on which part of the disc a file is located.

File extension	The suffix following the period in a filename. Windows uses this to identify the source application program. For example .mdb indicates an Access file.
Filename	The name given to a file. In Windows 95 and above this can be up to 256 characters long.
Filter	A set of criteria that is applied to data to show a subset of the data.
Firewall	Security measures designed to protect a networked system from unauthorised access.
Floppy disc	A removable disc on which information can be stored magnetically.
Folder	An area used to store a group of files, usually with a common link.
Font	A graphic design representing a set of characters, numbers and symbols.
Freeware	Software that is available for downloading and unlimited use without charge.
FTP	File Transfer Protocol. The procedure for connecting to a remote computer and transferring files.
Function key	One of the series of 10 or 12 keys marked with the letter F and a numeral, used for specific operations.
Gateway	A computer system that allows otherwise incompatible networks to communicate with each other.

GIF	Graphics Interchange Format, a common standard for images on the Web.
Graphic	A picture or illustration, also called an image. Formats include GIF, JPEG, BMP, PCX, and TIFF.
Graphics card	A device that controls the display on the monitor and other allied functions.
GUI	A Graphic User Interface, such as Windows 98, the software front-end meant to provide an attractive and easy to use interface.
Hard copy	Output on paper.
Hard disc	A device built into the computer for holding programs and data.
Hardware	The equipment that makes up a computer system, excluding the programs or software.
Help	A Windows system that gives you instructions and additional information on using a program.
Helper application	A program allowing you to view multimedia files that your web browser cannot handle internally.
Hit	A single request from a web browser for a single item from a web server.
Home page	The document displayed when you first open your Web browser, or the first document you come to at a Web site.
Host	Computer connected directly to the Internet that provides services to other local and/or remote computers.

Hotlist	A list of frequently used Web locations and URL addresses.
Host	A computer acting as an information or communications server.
HTML	HyperText Markup Language, the format used in documents on the Web.
HTML editor	Authoring tool which assists with the creation of HTML pages.
HTTP	HyperText Transport Protocol, the system used to link and transfer hypertext documents on the Web.
Hyperlink	A segment of text, or an image, that refers to another document on the Web, an Intranet or your PC.
Hypermedia	Hypertext extended to include linked multimedia.
Hypertext	A system that allows documents to be cross-linked so that the reader can explore related links, or documents, by clicking on a highlighted symbol.
Icon	A small graphic image that represents a function or object. Clicking on an icon produces an action.
Image	See graphic.
Insertion point	A flashing bar that shows where typed text will be entered into a document.
Interface	A device that allows you to connect a computer to its peripherals.
Internet	The global system of computer networks.

Intranet	A private network inside an organisation using the same kind of software as the Internet.
ISA	Industry Standard Architecture; a standard for internal connections in PCs.
ISDN	Integrated Services Digital Network, a telecom standard using digital transmission technology to support voice, video and data communications applications over regular telephone lines.
IP	Internet Protocol - The rules that provide basic Internet functions.
IP Address	Internet Protocol Address - every computer on the Internet has a unique identifying number.
ISP	Internet Service Provider - A company that offers access to the Internet.
Java	An object-oriented programming language created by Sun Microsystems for developing applications and applets that are capable of running on any computer, regardless of the operating system.
JPEG/JPG	Joint Photographic Experts Group, a popular cross-platform format for image files. JPEG is best suited for true colour original images.
Kilobyte	(KB); 1024 bytes of information or storage space.
LAN	Local Area Network - High-speed, privately-owned network covering a

	limited geographical area, such as an office or a building.
Laptop	A portable computer small enough to sit on your lap.
LCD	Liquid Crystal Display.
Links	The hypertext connections between Web pages.
Local	A resource that is located on your computer, not linked to it over a network.
Location	An Internet address.
Log on	To gain access to a network.
MCI	Media Control Interface - a standard for files and multimedia devices.
Megabyte	(MB); 1024 kilobytes of information or storage space.
Megahertz	(MHz); Speed of processor in millions of cycles per second.
Memory	Part of computer consisting of storage elements organised into addressable locations that can hold data and instructions.
Menu	A list of available options in an application.
Menu bar	The horizontal bar that lists the names of menus.
MIDI	Musical Instrument Digital Interface - enables devices to transmit and receive sound and music messages.
MIME	Multipurpose Internet Mail Extensions, a messaging standard that allows Internet users to exchange

	e-mail messages enhanced with graphics, video and voice.
MIPS	Million Instructions Per Second; measures speed of a system.
Modem	Short for Modulator-demodulator devices. An electronic device that lets computers communicate electronically.
Monitor	The display device connected to your PC, also called a screen.
Mouse	A device used to manipulate a pointer around your display and activate processes by pressing buttons.
MPEG	Motion Picture Experts Group - a video file format offering excellent quality in a relatively small file.
MS-DOS	Microsoft's implementation of the Disc Operating System for PCs.
Multimedia	The use of photographs, music and sound and movie images in a presentation.
Multi-tasking	Performing more than one operation at the same time.
Network	Two or more computers connected together to share resources.
Network server	Central computer which stores files for several linked computers.
Node	Any single computer connected to a network.
ODBC	Open DataBase Connectivity - A standard protocol for accessing information in a SQL database server.

OLE	Object Linking and Embedding - A technology for transferring and sharing information among software applications.
Online	Having access to the Internet.
On-line Service	Services such as America On-line and CompuServe that provide content to subscribers and usually connections to the Internet.
Operating system	Software that runs a computer.
Page	An HTML document, or Web site.
Password	A unique character string used to gain access to a network, program, or mailbox.
PATH	The location of a file in the directory tree.
Peripheral	Any device attached to a PC.
Perl	A popular language for programming CGI applications.
PIF file	Program information file - gives information to Windows about an MS-DOS application.
Pixel	A picture element on screen; the smallest element that can be independently assigned colour and intensity.
Plug-and-play	Hardware which can be plugged into a PC and be used immediately without configuration.
POP	Post Office Protocol - a method of storing and returning e-mail.
Port	The place where information goes into or out of a computer, e.g. a

	modem might be connected to the serial port.
PPP	Point-to-Point Protocol - One of two methods (see SLIP) for using special software to establish a temporary direct connection to the Internet over regular phone lines.
Print queue	A list of print jobs waiting to be sent to a printer.
Program	A set of instructions which cause a computer to perform tasks.
Protocol	A set of rules or standards that define how computers communicate with each other.
Query	The set of keywords and operators sent by a user to a search engine, or a database search request.
Queue	A list of e-mail messages waiting to be sent over the Internet.
RAM	Random Access Memory. The computer's volatile memory. Data held in it is lost when power is switched off.
Real mode	MS-DOS mode, typically used to run programs, such as MS-DOS games, that will not run under Windows.
Resource	A directory, or printer, that can be shared over a network.
Robot	A Web agent that visits sites, by requesting documents from them, for the purposes of indexing for search engines. Also known as Wanderers, Crawlers, or Spiders.
ROM	Read Only Memory. A PC's non-volatile memory. Data is written

	into this memory at manufacture and is not affected by power loss.
Scroll bar	A bar that appears at the right side or bottom edge of a window.
Search	Submit a query to a search engine.
Search engine	A program that helps users find information across the Internet.
Serial interface	An interface that transfers data as individual bits.
Server	A computer system that manages and delivers information for client computers.
Shared resource	Any device, program or file that is available to network users.
Shareware	Software that is available on public networks and bulletin boards. Users are expected to pay a nominal amount to the software developer.
Signature file	An ASCII text file, maintained within e-mail programs, that contains text for your signature.
Site	A place on the Internet. Every Web page has a location where it resides which is called its site.
SLIP	Serial Line Internet Protocol, a method of Internet connection that enables computers to use phone lines and a modem to connect to the Internet without having to connect to a host.
SMTP	Simple Mail Transfer Protocol - a protocol dictating how e-mail messages are exchanged over the Internet.

Socket	An endpoint for sending and receiving data between computers.
Software	The programs and instructions that control your PC.
Spamming	Sending the same message to a large number of mailing lists or newsgroups. Also to overload a Web page with excessive keywords in an attempt to get a better search ranking.
Spider	See robot.
Spooler	Software which handles transfer of information to a store to be used by a peripheral device.
SQL	Structured Query Language, used with relational databases.
SSL	Secure Sockets Layer, the standard transmission security protocol developed by Netscape, which has been put into the public domain.
Subscribe	To become a member of.
Surfing	The process of looking around the Internet.
SVGA	Super Video Graphics Array; it has all the VGA modes but with 256, or more, colours.
Swap file	An area of your hard disc used to store temporary operating files, also known as virtual memory.
Sysop	System Operator - A person responsible for the physical operations of a computer system or network resource.

System disc	A disc containing files to enable a PC to start up.
T1	An Internet leased line that carries up to 1.536 million bits per second (1.536Mbps).
T3	An Internet leased line that carries up to 45 million bits per second (45Mbps).
TCP/IP	Transmission Control Protocol/Internet Protocol, combined protocols that perform the transfer of data between two computers. TCP monitors and ensures the correct transfer of data. IP receives the data, breaks it up into packets, and sends it to a network within the Internet.
Telnet	A program which allows people to remotely use computers across networks.
Text file	An unformatted file of text characters saved in ASCII format.
Thread	An ongoing message-based conversation on a single subject.
TIFF	Tag Image File Format - a popular graphic image file format.
Tool	Software program used to support Web site creation and management.
Toolbar	A bar containing icons giving quick access to commands.
Toggle	To turn an action on and off with the same switch.
TrueType fonts	Fonts that can be scaled to any size and print as they show on the screen.

UNC	Universal Naming Convention - A convention for files that provides a machine independent means of locating the file that is particularly useful in Web based applications.
UNIX	Multitasking, multi-user computer operating system that is run by many computers that are connected to the Internet.
Upload/Download	The process of transferring files between computers. Files are uploaded from your computer to another and downloaded from another computer to your own.
URL	Uniform Resource Locator, the addressing system used on the Web, containing information about the method of access, the server to be accessed and the path of the file to be accessed.
Usenet	Informal network of computers that allow the posting and reading of messages in newsgroups that focus on specific topics.
User ID	The unique identifier, usually used in conjunction with a password, which identifies you on a computer.
Virtual Reality	Simulations of real or imaginary worlds, rendered on a flat two-dimensional screen but appearing three-dimensional.
Virus	A malicious program, downloaded from a web site or disc, designed to wipe out information on your computer.

W3C

The World Wide Web Consortium that is steering standards development for the Web.

WAIS

Wide Area Information Server, a Net-wide system for looking up specific information in Internet databases.

WAV

Waveform Audio (.wav) - a common audio file format for DOS/Windows computers.

Web

A network of hypertext-based multimedia information servers. Browsers are used to view any information on the Web.

Web Page

An HTML document that is accessible on the Web.

Webmaster

One whose job it is to manage a web site.

WINSOCK

A Microsoft Windows file that provides the interface to TCP/IP services.

Wizard

A Microsoft tool that asks you questions and then creates an object depending on your answers.

Index

A

Access database 199
Accessing
   Control Panel 5
   date and time 86
   menus 26
Activating commands 26
Active
   printer 72
   window 20
Adding
   buttons 58
   movies and sound 177
   page theme 176
Add/Remove
   programs 5
   toolbar buttons 212
Address
   book 166
   list 196
Aligning
   outline levels 142
   paragraphs 79
   text 79
Alignment
   buttons 79
   commands 79
   pointers 36
Animate command 106
Annotations 7, 87
Application
   command button 20
   icons 20
   starting 19
Arrow 139
Assembling long doc's 151

Attaching
   file to e-mail 165
   macro to toolbar 205
Auto
   backup 50
   caption 8
   correct 7, 12
   format 7, 9
   number 103
   shapes 116
   summarise 10
   text 29
   update 86

B

Backspace key 57
Backup copy 50
Blocks of text 59
Bold 78
Border button 24
Boxes
   dialogue 32
   list 33
   text 106, 111
Breaks
   page 29, 66
   paragraph 79
Built-in templates 43, 93
Bullet
   buttons 24
   insert 9, 85
Buttons
   assign macro 205
   command 20
   font 24
   minimise 20, 21

on Formatting bar 22, 24
on Standard toolbar 23
on Status bar 25
outline 144
restore 20, 21
Start 3, 19
style 43
tab setting 89
What's this? 39

C
Carriage return
find & replace 65
hard 65
Centre
align button 79
aligned tabs 89
command 79
Changing
active window 20
character format 96
column format 104
default options 47, 50
font 65
menu commands 215
page layout 49
paper size 47
paragraph styles 43
paper source 49
text 63
view(s) 20, 44
Character
font 65
formatting 96
Chart
arrows 139
create 135
data 135
enhancement 139
text box 139
types 137

Check
boxes 34
grammar 7, 69
spelling 7, 10, 67
synonyms 68
Clean screen 9, 46
Clip Art / Gallery 189
Clipboard 12
Close
button 20, 21
document 55
file 55
window 20, 21
Column width 126
Columns 104
Comments 7
Command buttons 21
Commands shortcut 31
Communication ports 72
Context sensitive help 37
Control Panel 5, 157
Copy
blocks of text 61
command 31, 58
information 184
text button 23
toolbar buttons 212
Correcting text 7, 57
Creating
address list 196
backup copy 50
bulleted list button 85
bulleted lists 85
charts 8, 135
custom toolbar 213
document template 93
drawing 8, 117
footer 101
footnote 103
glossary 7
header 101

index 146
macro 201
new docum't button 55
new folder 52
outline 141
paragraph styles 43, 91
style 91
table 8, 124
table of contents 146
text boxes 106, 111
Web pages 172
Current
date 86
font 24
font size 24, 76
paragraph style 43
point size 24
ruler 20
style 90
Cursor movement 42
Custom toolbar 213
Customising
Assistant 17
menus 210
toolbars 210
Cut
command 31, 58
text button 58

D
Date insert 86
Decimal tabs 89
Decrease indent 81
Default
display 20
menus 210
options 47, 50
printer 72
style box 43
toolbar buttons 20
toolbars 210

view 50
Define style 91
Delete
files 148
key 57
text 62
Demote paragraph 143
Dialogue boxes 36
Dictionaries 67
Display modes 44
Document
annotation 87
basics 41
checking 67
closing 55
command button 20
copying 61
editing 57
e-mail 158
enhancements 99
formatting 75
navigation 42
opening button 56
preview 74
properties 54
printing 71
save command 51
screen displays 44
styles 90
templates 93
views 20, 44
Double line spacing 80
Drag & Drop
hyperlinks 170
text 7, 61, 62
Draw
button 115
table commands 8
Drawing
create 117
edit 117

layered objects	118
text box	115
Tool	115
toolbar	116

E

Edit

command	28
copy/cut/paste	58
document	57
find	34, 63
go to	42
macro	207
table	131
undo	63, 75

Editing

documents	57
drawing	117
embedded objects	192
hyperlinks	170
macros	207

E-mail 155

button	23
documents	14, 158
header buttons	162
signatures	163

Embedding

file	190
objects	9, 189

Embolding command	78
Endnotes	103
Enhancements	78
Enlarged view	44, 46
Entering text	41
Equation editor	119
Eraser tool	8
Excel worksheet	185
Explorer	168
Expressions	127

F

File

attachment	165
close	55
command	26, 28
delete	148
exit	28
find	148
location	53
management	148
menu	26, 28
names	52
new	34, 55, 57
open	32, 55
page setup	47
preview	74
print	71
properties	72
save	50, 51
save as	51
save as Web page	173
send to	158
transfer protocol	1
types	52

Web page view 172

Find

file	10, 148
help	37

Find & Replace	25, 63
Font box	78, 96
Fonts	76
Footers	101
Footnotes	103

Format

command	29
text box	111
theme	92

Formatting

bar	20, 22, 24
borders	23
buttons	24

characters 75
columns 104
documents 75
features 96
toolbar 24
page tabs 89
paragraphs 83
quick keys 79
styles 90
tables 133
tabs 89
text 75
toolbar 24
Formulae 127
Frame
creation 8
layering 118
Frames 105
FTP 1, 180
Full screen mode 46
Functions in tables 130

G
Getting address list 198
Go To command 25, 42
Grammar checker 7, 11, 69
Graph 134

H
Handles (text boxes) 107
Hanging indents 82
Hard
disc space 2
page break 66
Hardware requirements 2
Headers 101
Headings styles 9, 43
Help
command 31
index 38
macros 208

menu 37
toolbars and menus 217
Highlight text 78
Horizontal scroll bar 20
HTML
differences 178
file format 1, 153
Hypertext links 11, 167
Hyphens 12, 98

I
Import graphic 112
Increase indent 81
Indentation 81
buttons 24
Index creation 146
Insert
annotations 87
bullets 85
characters 97
charts 134
command 29
comments 87
date and time 86
equation 120
Excel worksheet 187
footnotes 7, 103
formula 127
graphs 134
hyperlinks 23, 167
hyphens 98
mode 58
objects 119, 134
page break 66
page layout 49
page numbers 99
picture 112, 189
subdocument 151
symbols 97, 104
table 123
text boxes 106

Insertion point	20, 23	help	208
Installing Office 2000	3	playback	204
IntelliSense	7	record	201
Internet Web pages	171	remove	206
ISP	156	run	204
Italicise command	78	save	203
		Mail merge	193
J		Managing files	148
Justified		Margins	47
align button	79	Mark text	10
		Master document	151
K		Maximise button	20, 21
Keyboard		Memory requirement	2
shortcut keys	78	Menu bar	20, 21, 26
text selection	59	Merging	
		lists	193
L		table cells	126, 131
Landscape orientation	48	Microsoft	
Large documents	141	Chart	134
Layered drawings	118	Clip Gallery	112, 189
Layout		Draw	115
page mode	49	Equation	120
table	124	Graph	134
Leader characters	90	Minimise button	20, 21
Left		Modes	
align button	79	draw	115
aligned tabs	89	page layout	49
command	79	master document	151
Levels of outline	142	outline	141
Linking		Modify	
file	190	margins	47
objects	9, 188	style	92
List boxes	33	Mouse pointer(s)	20, 35
Long documents	141	Moving	
LPT1 port	72	around document	42
		blocks of text	62
M		information	184
Macro		text boxes	107
attach to Toolbar	205	toolbar buttons	212
create / record	201	toolbars	77
edit	207	Multiple columns	104

N
Navigation shortcuts 42
New
   features 12
   file 55, 57
   window 31
Normal
   mode 44
   layout 44
   paragraph style 43
   style 90
   template 43
   view 44
Number of columns 104
Numbered
   list 9, 85
   outline 142
Numbering pages 99

O
Object
   creation 8
   link and embed 188
   type 119
Office
   applications 5
   Art 8, 112
   Assistant 15, 17, 37
   clipboard 12
   Help 37
OLE 1, 183, 188
Online help 15, 37
Open
   document button 23
   file button 55
Opening files 10, 56
Option buttons 34
Orientation of text 48, 112
Outlook 2000 155
Outline
   assigning levels 142

   buttons 144
   layout 45
   levels 142
   mode 45, 141
   numbering 145
   view 142
Overtype mode 58

P
Page
   breaks 29, 66
   columns 104
   set-up command 47
   layout 49
   margins 47
   numbering 99
   orientation 48
   set-up 47
   tabs 89
Paper settings 47
Paragraph
   alignment 79
   formatting 83
   marks 79
   spacing 80
   styles 43, 91
Parallel printer port 72
Paste
   button 23
   command 31, 58
Pattern matching 64
Pause macro button 203
Personalised stationery 164
Picture
   bar 114
   importing 112
Playback macro 204
Point size 24, 76
Pointer(s) 20, 35
Portrait orientation 48
Ports 72

Pre-defined charts 137
Preview
   document 8, 74
   file 150
Print
   command / button 23, 72
   document / files 71
   layout 45
   master document 152
   options 73
   orientation 48, 73
   previews 74
   settings 50
Printer
   icon 72
   ports 72
   settings 71
Promote paragraph 143
Properties 54
Pull down menus 26

Q
Quick key formatting 79

R
RAM requirement 2
Record macro 201
Remove
   macro 206
   toolbar buttons 212
Rename files 148
Reference mark 103
Repair Office 2000 6
Replacing text 63
Restore
   button 20, 21
   default menus 216
   default toolbars 216
Right
   align button 79
   command 79

   aligned tabs 89
Row height 126
Ruler area 20, 22
Run
   command 3
   macros 204

S
Save As
   command 51
   type 52
Save
   button / command 23, 51
   macro 203
   options 50, 51
   Web pages 179
Screen 20
Screen displays 44
Scroll arrows / bars 20, 22
Search & replace 25, 63
Select browse object 20
Selecting
   object 119
   style 90
   table cells 135
   text 59
Selection bar 20, 23
Set tab buttons 89
Set-up printer 72
Sharing information 183
Shortcut
   keys 79
   menus 7, 31
Signatures (e-mail) 163
Single line spacing 80
Size
   paper 47
   text box 111
Soft page break 66
Software requirements 2
Sort file lists 150

Spacing paragraphs 80
Special
    characters 97
    formatting 96
Spell checker 7, 67
Split
    box 20, 22
    table cells 131
Standard toolbar 20, 22, 23
Start
    button 3, 19
    menu 4
    MS-Draw 115
    MS-Graph 134
Starting Word 19
Status bar 20, 23, 25
Stop macro button 203
Style
    basics 90
    box 43
    create 91
    formatting 90
    modify 92
    paragraph 91
Sub / Superscript 78
Symbols 97
Synonyms 68
System settings 157

T
Tab
    key 89
    leader 90
    types 89
Table
    autoformat 133
    button 124
    column width 126
    command 30
    creation 8, 124
    editing 131

    formatting 133
    formulae 127
    functions 130
    insert 124
    layout 124
    merge cells 131
    navigation 125
    of contents 146
    operators 130
    properties 127
    row height 126
    selection 135
    split cells 131
Templates 10, 43, 93
Text
    alignment 79
    boxes 106, 111
    copying 61
    correction 57
    deleting 62
    direction 112
    Drag & Drop 7, 61, 62
    editing 58
    enhancement 78
    entering 41
    finding & replacing 63
    formatting 75
    formatting shortcuts 78
    indentation 81
    moving 62
    rotation 112
    selection 59
    searching 63
Text box
    creation 105
    handles 110
    insertion 106
    moving 107
    sizing 111
Thesaurus 68
Time insert 86

Title bar   20, 21
Toolbar   20, 23
Toolbar buttons   20
Tools
  command   30
  drawing   114
  macro command   204
  options   36, 50

U
Underline command   78
Undo
  buttons   23
  command   63, 75
Units of measurement   81
Update
  date and time   86
  links   28
User dictionary   67
Using
  footnotes   103
  headers and footers   101
  Grammar checker   7, 69
  Help menu   37
  hypertext links   167
  layered drawings   118
  multiple columns   104
  Office Assistant   15
  signatures   163
  Spell checker   7, 67
  Thesaurus   7, 68
  Web page wizard   173

V
Vertical scroll bar   20
Versioning feature   11
Video clip   192
View
  button   149
  clean screen   9, 46
  command   28, 44

comments   7
footnotes   103
full screen mode   46
header/footer   101
master document   151
merge data icon   200
normal mode   44
options   50
outline mode   45
page layout   49
paragraph marks   79
print mode   45
ruler   22
toolbars   77, 210
Web mode   44
Views
  button(s)   20, 23, 149
  menu   150
Visual Basic   1, 201, 209

W
Web
  browser button   16
  folders   13, 179
  layout   13, 44
Web page   11, 171
  movies and sound   177
  template   174
  theme   13, 176
  wizard   13, 173
What's this? button   39
Window
  active   20
  close button   20, 21
  command   31, 55
Word
  address list   196
  Art   94
  chart   134
  default options   50
  document   41

environment	19
features	7, 12
general settings	50
help button	23
icon	19
macros	201
screen	20
wrap	41
Word Mail templates	11
WordPerfect user help	9
WYSIWYG	1

Z
Zoom	44, 46

Companion Discs

COMPANION DISCS are available for most computer books written by the same author(s) and published by BERNARD BABANI (publishing) LTD, as listed at the front of this book (except for those marked with an asterisk). These books contain many pages of file/program listings. There is no reason why you should spend hours typing them into your computer, unless you wish to do so, or need the practice.

ORDERING INSTRUCTIONS

To obtain companion discs, fill in the order form below, or a copy of it, enclose a cheque (payable to **P.R.M. Oliver**) or a postal order, and send it to the address given below. **Make sure you fill in your name and address** and specify the book number and title in your order.

Book No.	Book Name	Unit Price	Total Price
BP		£3.50	
BP		£3.50	
BP		£3.50	
Name		Sub-total	£.............
Address		P & P (@ 45p/disc)	£.............
		Total Due	£.............

Send to: P.R.M. Oliver, CSM, Pool, Redruth, Cornwall, TR15 3SE

PLEASE NOTE

The author(s) are fully responsible for providing this Companion Disc service. The publishers of this book accept no responsibility for the supply, quality, or magnetic contents of the disc, or in respect of any damage, or injury that might be suffered or caused by its use.